A BANTAM PATHFINDER EDITION

"You know, I've often said that every poem
solves something for me in life. I go so far
as to say that every poem is a momentary
stay against the confusion of the world."

ROBERT FROST viewed poetry as a performance,
a retreat, an act of love to the world,
a protest. In the development of his great
poetic themes, he achieved a depth and
complexity sometimes obscured by his popular
image. He defied classification, delighting
in his "uncatchability," as he once called it.

Through an illustrated biography,
interpretations, and the poems themselves,
this book brings the man and the poet
vividly to life.

FROST
THE POET AND HIS POETRY

DAVID A. SOHN
Curriculum Coordinator of English
and Social Studies, District 65,
Cook County, Evanston, Illinois

RICHARD H. TYRE
Coordinator of Humanities,
Abington High School,
Abington, Pennsylvania

SPECIAL REVISED EDITION

BANTAM  BOOKS

BANTAM PATHFINDER EDITIONS
NEW YORK / TORONTO / LONDON

FROST

The Poet and His Poetry

RLI: $\dfrac{\text{VLM } 7.0}{\text{IL } 7.12}$

FROST: THE POET AND HIS POETRY
*A Bantam Book / published by arrangement with
Holt, Rinehart and Winston, Inc.*

*Bantam Pathfinder edition published April 1969
2nd printing
3rd printing*

*Bantam Books are published by Bantam Books, Inc., a subsidiary
of Grosset & Dunlap, Inc. Its trade-mark, consisting of the words
"Bantam Books" and the portrayal of a bantam, is registered in the
United States Patent Office and in other countries. Marca Registrada.
Bantam Books, Inc., 271 Madison Avenue, New York, N.Y. 10016.*

PRINTED IN THE UNITED STATES OF AMERICA

Contents

His head carved out of granite O,
His hair a wayward drift of snow,
He worshipped the great God of Flow
By holding on and letting go.

From "In Memoriam: Four Poets" by Robert
Francis, from the book, Come Out Into The
Sun, University of Massachusetts Press.

If Robert Frost was much honored dur-
ing his lifetime, it was because a good
many preferred to ignore his darker
truths.

John F. Kennedy, in the film
A Lover's Quarrel with the World.

Introduction

To study Robert Frost, the man and the poet, is to engage in a challenging and rewarding investigation of a complex personality and a subtle, brilliant artist. Because he consciously created an image of simplicity through both his poetry and his public appearances, the dimensions and the depth of Robert Frost will come as a surprise to many readers.

Frost viewed poetry as performance; he probably felt the same way about the act of living itself. As a performer he wore many varied masks, delighting in the deception of his "uncatchability," as he once called it. He warned readers that it was a mistake to read too much into his poetry or to identify him with the speakers in his poems.

Hidden behind Frost's deception lay his depth—his veiled ideas.

> I began my first poem with a cause. Sometimes I come too near the surface with the cause—usually I keep it buried. Still in my books, but veiled, but still there.[1]

An interviewer tried to pin him down and classify him, but later said:

> Let me put it this way: Imagine that you see a butterfly, and its beauty is something you want to capture and take home with you. You catch the butterfly and place it carefully on a cardboard under glass. And to your sorrow, you haven't caught the butterfly at all. . . . Where once the butterfly had a subtle, vibrant aliveness, the very act of pinning it down has destroyed it for you.[2]

Frost resisted labels. On NBC's *Conversation* program, the interviewer stated that authors and critics had labeled him a nature poet, a New England Yankee, symbolist, humanist, and other things. Which did he consider true?

"I take 'em all. Take 'em and put my arms around 'em," he said. By embracing them all, he avoided each of them.

The stereotyped portrait of Robert Frost is for many that of a "Farmer Brown," a poet who loved nature and wrote affectionately about it.

John Ciardi, poet and friend, summed up concisely his objection to this cliché when he objected to a film about Frost made by the United States Information Service that painted the stereotyped picture of him. Frost asked him why he did not like the film. Ciardi replied, "Because . . . Robert Frost is no lollipop." Continuing in his editorial, Ciardi explained: "No man makes it into the dimensions of a Robert Frost on simple sweetness. There is not that much combustion in sugar."[3]

Although there are many other aspects of the stereotype that are misleading, perhaps the following account will demonstrate how dangerous such over-simplification can be.

In the same *Conversation* program, Frost denied that he was a nature poet. "I guess I'm not a nature poet," he said. "I've only written two poems without a human being in them. Only two."

He then proceeded to answer the question: Is nature essentially kind? "I know it isn't kind. Matthew Arnold said, 'Nature is cruel. It's man that's sick of blood.' And man doesn't seem so very sick of it. Nature is always more or less cruel."

Frost. family, and friends on a Vermont Sunday afternoon.

The fact that Frost regarded nature as cruel may come as a surprise to many readers. It is a common misconception about the poet. This book attempts to provide insights into both the man and the poet through his poetry and through his own statements about himself in letters and in conversations with friends. The section on his life that follows emphasizes the period from his birth in 1874 to 1915, the year he returned from England with his family. It was during these early years that the poet perfected his art and wrote much of his best work.

Complex and enigmatic, Frost offers for the reader the force of his engaging personality and the impact of some of the best poetry an American has ever written.

I

Frost: The Man

1874

Robert Lee Frost was born in San Francisco, California, March 26, the son of William Prescott Frost, Jr., of Lawrence, Massachusetts, and Isabelle Moodie Frost, of Edinburgh, Scotland.

Where you come from is of very great importance, you know, your family ways. I was brought up and started life in San Francisco. My father was chairman of the Democratic city committee when Cleveland was elected. I never went to school until I was about twelve years old and I wasn't very well; and I went downtown with my father all the time, had all my noon meals with him in the big headquarters of the Democratic Party saloon—Abe Levy's saloon—and I was sort of political kid round.[4]

Robert's father [wrote Untermeyer], a doggedly honest Democrat in a corrupt and hypocritical Republican state, had offended the self-righteous community by rejecting ritual and refusing to go to church. His mother, on the other hand, was a confirmed true believer. Born a Scotch Presbyterian, she became a Unitarian; . . . after studying Emerson . . . she became a Swedenborgian.

Robert inherited these mixed tendencies. He began as a romantic affirmer (not, he emphasized, a reformer), and became a nonconformist.[5]

The first school I went to at his age [Frost's grandchild's] was in San Francisco along about fifteen years after the Civil War . . . I cried (wept) myself out of that first school in one day . . . on general principles. I didn't get back again for two years. I've been jumping school ever since.[6]

Sometimes a person's real character is slow in blossoming. Until I was fourteen I had never read a book. I thought, and those who knew me thought, I was more mechanically minded than anything else. But after I had read my first book a new world opened up for me, and after that I devoured as many of them as I could lay my hands on. By the time I was fifteen I was already beginning to write verses.[7]

Apart from home, there were other influences on the young Frost—notably, his initiation into Seth Balsa's gang. It was no contest. By the time Seth Balsa had seen enough and had stepped in to separate the warriors, one of Percy's eyes was well marked; but Robbie's nose was bleeding, both of his cheeks were bloody, and his lower lip was badly split. Nevertheless, the Washington Street gang had been impressed by Robbie's courage, and Balsa welcomed him into full membership before sending him home to get his face patched up.

Painfully hurt, and on the verge of tears, Rob jumped down from the Washington Street retaining wall and started home, filled with misery and elation. He had not expected that he would have to pay such a price and take such a beating. But before he reached 1404 Leavenworth Street, he began telling himself that this was the most important day in his life so far. His courage had conquered his cowardice. Suddenly he had grown up.[8]

1885

Frost moved to Lawrence, Massachusetts, with his mother and sister after the death of his father. I came East—and my mother'd leave us at Omaha and at Chicago to re-check my father's coffin, me and my sister—I was twelve years old.[9]

1890

At age sixteen he published his first poem, "La Noche Triste," in the Lawrence High School "Bulletin." I recall how there was a wind and a darkness. I had never written a poem before, and as I walked, it appeared like a revelation, and I became so taken by it that I was late at my grandmother's.[10]

1892

Frost graduated from Lawrence High School and was co-valedictorian with his future wife. I didn't know I was head of the class of 1892. In the second year they began to play it on me. In the third year it became a school issue and I was in distress. There was a rivalry between the Greek and Latin teachers,

Elinor Miriam White

Robert Lee Frost

and Elinor bobbed up in the last year as a rival. The head of the school was a very cultivated man, Greek and Latin scholar, aware of the "higher uncertainties." I had him only in Greek and Roman history. This head of school came to me, smoked as a ham, scholarly and lazy—very pleasant.

"Do you realize," he said to me, "that Miss White is catching up—she may get the valedictory?"

I said: "Give it to her now." No he wouldn't, but called it a tie. So Elinor, too, gave a speech.[11]

Frost studied at Dartmouth College. None of my relatives wanted me to write. Grandfather wanted me to be a lawyer. My mother was very fond of poetry, and, while she never said so, I always felt that underneath she wanted me to write. So I entered college. While my marks were always good, I somehow felt that I was wasting time. . . .[12]

Tuition was low, $90.00 a year. Mine was only $10.00 because I had won a fellowship, and because I was a monitor and because I did not stay even a whole term. My room in Wentworth Hall was $26.00 a year, and my board was $2.50 a week.

There was no drinking at all—if we wanted an orgy, we sat up all night with a box of Turkish paste [a gummy candy covered with confectioner's sugar].

I was invited into a fraternity—Theta Delta Chi—and joined up. One of my "rich" classmates paid my initiation fee. But somehow I was no fraternity brother.

No housekeeper either; the rooms in Wentworth were heated by open coal stoves. I never emptied my ashes—just let them pile up on the floor till they reached the door. My mother had to send up my high-school friend Carl Burrell from Lawrence to dig me out.

I had a large indifference to my teachers. I guess I

9

wanted to be a teacher myself and be on top—not underneath the system. Instinctively, I suppose.[13]

Rob fell more and more [said Elizabeth Sergeant] into long walks, night and day walks in the fine woods and hills that surround Hanover. Night walks were never scary to him—it was in a house that he felt afraid sometimes. His unsocial way puzzled the Theta Delts, and he was finally visited by a delegation of wags who asked what he did in the woods—*all alone*.

"I gnaw wood," was his reply.[14]

He left Dartmouth without notice, without taking his term examinations, and without saying good-bye. I was glad to seize the excuse (to myself) that my mother needed me in her school, to take care of some big, brutal boys she could not manage.

That wasn't the real reason. I had decided I was up to no good at Dartmouth, so I just went home to Methuen.[15]

1894

Twilight, *Frost's first volume of poetry, was printed privately in Lawrence, Mass. He collected the poems especially for Elinor and paid for their publication himself. "My Butterfly," his first professionally published poem, was printed in the* Independent, *a weekly literary magazine of that period.* The entire edition consisted of two leather-bound copies, one for Elinor White, the other for himself. But when his fiancée seemed insufficiently impressed by the gift, and also seemed to be showing interest in several suitors at St. Lawrence University, Frost despondently destroyed his own copy of the book. Immediately thereafter he struck an even more dramatic posture of despondency when he tried to throw his life away in unconvincing fashion by making a mysterious trip to and through the Dismal Swamp of Virginia.[16]

"My Butterfly" was written when Frost was nine-teen. "I wrote it," R. F. told me [Elizabeth Sergeant], "all in one go in the kitchen of our house in Tremont Street. I locked the door and all the time I was work-ing, Jeanie, my sister, tried to batter it down and get in."

Even as he wrote it he had "sensed in a way that something was happening. It was like cutting along a nerve." He read me the first two stanzas to illustrate:

MY BUTTERFLY

Thine emulous fond flowers are dead, too,
And the daft sun-assaulter, he
That frighted thee so oft, is fled or dead:
Save only me
(Nor is it sad to thee!)
Save only me
There is none left to mourn thee in the fields.

The gray grass is scarce dappled with the snow;
Its two banks have not shut upon the river;
But it is long ago—
It seems forever—
Since first I saw thee glance,
With all thy dazzling other ones,
In airy dalliance,
Precipitate in love,
Tossed, tangled, whirled and whirled above,
Like a limp rose-wreath in a fairy dance.

"The first stanza—well, that's nothing. But the sec-ond—it's as good as anything I've ever written. It was the beginning of *me*.

Its two banks have not shut upon the river;

"I got something there, and I knew it. But especially the last figure:

Like a limp rose-wreath in a fairy dance.

"That's like a blush. Never thought of that before. Poetry is like a cry, I've said. But it's like a blush—you can get something you didn't know you had." [17]

1895

At age twenty-one Robert Frost married Elinor Miriam White and taught in his mother's private school. Clara Searle (Mrs. H. K. Painter of Minneapolis) recalls the young Frost in his early teaching role. Under Robert Frost himself I studied arithmetic. Two rooms across the center of the house formed the classroom. There must have been about twenty pupils. Above the fireplace was a blackboard on which were written each day poems, short and long. Into notebooks we copied the poems and we learned them by heart. . . . A door from the family dining room opened directly into this bay, our arithmetic was the first class of the morning, and as we sat and waited, the door finally opened and the blue-eyed young man seated himself casually at the desk. The aroma of toast still associates itself in my mind with arithmetic. . . .

"I can't understand it, I can't, I can't!" I insisted stubbornly and with some heat.

"Yes you can, Clara Searle, if you want to, but you have made up your mind that you won't see it," came back at me with some impatience and a great deal of truth.[18]

1897–1899

Frost was an undergraduate student at Harvard. In the sophomore year, though I had won a big scholarship, nothing went well. I know now why—Harvard had taken me away from the question whether I could write or not. . . . I got very sick, terribly so, as if something were very wrong with heart or stomach. Trouble in the solar plexus. So I resigned from the sophomore class at the end of March, to the Dean's regret. The doctor thought I would die. He sent me home to die.[19]

I seemed without pride or even without self-respect in those days; I didn't care what I was looked down on for doing. You see the danger of distorting me into too humble a beginning. I always had the keys of the city to play with so as not to take big things too seriously. I walked out of two colleges like nothing at all. I was no rebel. I must have left from failure to see the difference between being intellectual in college and being intellectual outside of college. I got suspicious that it was very much up to me to find out for myself whether I had it in me to write and think. I was shifting my dependence, you might say, from teachers to writers who had written before me.[20]

The Frosts went to live and work on a small farm. Elinor [writes Elizabeth Sergeant] was the one who solved the puzzle of what to do about a living. Downing her pride, in her high Puritan way, she went to Rob's widowed Grandfather Frost. Would he buy them a farm? One they had found for themselves, only twelve miles from Lawrence, in West Derry, Rockingham County, New Hampshire. Thirty acres rather run down and poor, but with orchard, fields, pasture, woodland, and spring. A one-man, one-horse farm. It cost $1,800. If Rob could get well enough to farm and write poetry, he might achieve this in Derry.

"Shall I give you a year?" [my grandfather asked me about then]. "I know what you are up to" [he meant poetry]. "Will you settle down if I give you a year to try this out?"

I struck a great auctioneer's pose and dared him with:

"Give me twenty, give me twenty!"

And that . . . is just what it took.[21]

To Rob it seemed at times that his wife and grand-father must have arrived at a secret agreement that this Derry venture would not last long, that not many months would pass before another grave would be dug and filled. His physical exhaustion, brought on by even a minimum of work in collecting eggs, carry-ing water, scattering grain was enough to make him prey to a welter of annoyances which aroused new resentments.[22]

1900–1909

Frost farmed and wrote poetry near West Derry, Rockingham County, New Hampshire. And we had a farm where I could *partly* earn a living—didn't do it very well. And I never was away from the farm an evening in more than three years, I think it was. Prob-ably it was. I think once I came home as late as eight o'clock. We never went to church, never went to any-thing. And there was nothing we were missing; we were having a very nice time. Nice little farm. And children. We had orchards and fruit and horse and cow and all that.

I only left it, drifted away from it for part-time teaching because I wasn't *quite* earning a living.[23]

Self-abasement and guilt accumulated in him until it became a despairing kind of self-hatred. Over-whelmed, he found that he didn't even want to strug-gle any longer against the waves of pain and sickness which washed over him. And why wait for this linger-ing death when there were easier ways to the same end. Each time he drove from his farm with his old horse and wagon along the back-country road to Derry Depot for provisions, he passed an isolated pond deep enough for drowning.[24]

Having reduced life to its lowest terms, and having been given the choice of death or life, he had found that he preferred to stay alive. More than that, he found that his irrational acts of caring and cherishing were signs of his willingness to settle for imperfection, including the wistfulness of loving one who might not love him as much as he loved her. Whatever the limitations of circumstance, including his health and his questionable capacities, he was ready to go about his business as hen-man and farmer and poet. There was at least the possibility of improvement, even as for him spring was such an improvement over winter.[25]

I might say the core of all my writing was probably the five free years I had there on the farm down the road a mile or two from Derry Village toward Lawrence. The only thing we had plenty of was time and seclusion. I couldn't have figured on it in advance. I hadn't that kind of foresight. But it turned out as right as a doctor's prescription.[26]

1906–1911

Frost taught, chiefly English, at Pinkerton Academy, Derry Village, New Hampshire, and wrote poetry. I was ambition-less, purposeless. For months on end I would do no work at all. I don't write because I wanted to write. I wrote because I wrote. I would exchange work with another farmer, perhaps during the haying, and for three weeks would sweat and toughen up. Then the hay fever would come on, and I would do no work until another haying.

During the entire eight years there was no friend ever sat down within our home. I'd have conversations from time to time with a trader interested in buying or selling a horse, or a poultry buyer. Friends never came. There were no friends. I sometimes think of those years as almost a fadeout . . . as an escape into a dream existence.[27]

We were in debt, and, somehow, coming to have

15

a prejudice against debt. It occurred to us that I might take up teaching again. I went to Lawrence and met on the street a minister named Wolcott, who'd taken a friendly interest in my mother and me years before. When my first poem was published, this minister sent for me, in part, I found, to congratulate me, but more to warn me. He was thinking of my mother. When I told him I was thinking of taking up teaching, he remarked there was an academy near me at Derry. He knew a minister who was one of the trustees, and he promised to write him.[28]

Reverend Merriam was sufficiently impressed to invite Rob to read a poem at the Men's League of the Congregational Church. . . . Such a gathering was more than Frost could face, but Mr. Merriam offered to read the poem. With grave misgivings for leaving his wife alone (only twice in eight years had he been away from Elinor in the evening), the arrangements were made.

"The Tuft of Flowers" (p. 102) was the offering, written for the occasion and read as a bid for a teaching position, "as little Tommy Tucker sang for his supper." On the strength of the poem, he was offered a part-time position teaching English at Pinkerton, which took him on at a bargain price, one-sixth of a thousand dollars for the year, to teach one class. "They got me cheap," Frost later said, but he didn't haggle over price. It was income.[29]

Poetry has got me indirectly or directly practically all the living I have had. It got me my job in Pinkerton then and got me into Amherst College later when I came home from England. . . . I worked many hours a week at Pinkerton; I should hardly dare to tell you how many. But many of them were as good hours as I ever had. . . . For two years I was only a part-time teacher. Then for three I taught a little more than anybody else, I think the records would show. But I never took my turn leading chapel. I was so obviously too scared they let me off—both the heads I came under, Mr. Bingham and Mr. Silver. I taught English chiefly, but also history, Latin, and geometry.

You might be interested to know that during my ten years in Derry, the first five of them farming altogether and the last five mostly teaching but still farming a little, I wrote more than half of my first book, much more than half of my second, and even quite a little of my third, though they were not published till later.[30]

In 1906 Frost entered the scene, not at a decorous walk, and never in time for chapel, but often at a gallop, taking the steps two at a time to reach his class. His hair, cut at home, was blown in all directions by the wind, and if that weren't enough, he'd run his fingers through the tousled locks defying any accidental order. His clothes were rumpled and ill-fitting. There were no indications that he made any effort to "spruce up" for the job. In class, unlike the ramrod-straight Miss Parsons who taught Greek or the stiff-collared Art Reynolds who taught history, Frost would slump down in his chair behind his desk, almost disappearing from sight except for his heavy-lidded eyes and bushy brows. In such a position Frost would "talk," or he might read aloud, or let a discussion go its own length. Teachers didn't know how to "take him," and students, accustomed to "prepared lessons," were inclined to think they could take advantage of a teacher who was not strict in the way they knew.

Frost felt his first year of teaching a failure.[31]

He did assign themes, contrary to later stories about his teaching methods, and any student willing to work would find helpful comments in the margin of his paper: "There, you have found the kind of thing you can do." "This really is an idea. The occasion is splendid. This seems to be done from life. What an interesting runaway." He'd ask questions as if he could learn something from them, an astonishing attitude for a teacher to take.[32]

Two of his students, John Bartlett and Margaret Abbott (whom Bartlett later married), became his lifelong friends. "I was a shy boy [said Bartlett]. In a matter-of-fact way Frost observed that I was a fellow who had ideas. That's all there was to the conversation, as a spinning ball came my way, but I can see Frost, the fall mud, and the football bucking machine. . . . He seemed to have several times the interest in me that other teachers had."

Gradually, this intensely personal, though never hurried, interest drew out the students, and Frost's judgment won their respect. An "A" from Frost became a coveted honor. . . .

He'd walk with John Bartlett down the country roads, covering a world of subjects in just a mile. If they came abreast of a logging team, Frost would stop and talk with the teamster about logging things, horses, and roads. Once they walked to Manchester, browsed for an hour in a bookstore, and then, fortifying themselves with oyster stew, rode the electric railway back to Derry. If the daylight ran out and the stars shone through the trees, it might be the occasion to discuss astronomy or Greek mythology; noticing a fern, Frost might observe that he hadn't seen one like it since he was last in the Lake Willoughby region; talk might be of present things, like baseball and football; or something could touch off reminiscences of his boyhood in industrial Lawrence. Rob never argued. He knew what he knew. And he would get his companion to talk, often about things he wasn't aware that he knew.[33]

Frost at homemade writing desk at Franconia, N.H., ca. 1915.

1911–1912

Frost taught psychology at New Hampshire State Normal School, Plymouth, New Hampshire.

1912–1915

Frost went to England with his wife and four children—Lesley, Carol, Irma, and Marjorie—and wrote and farmed in Buckinghamshire and Herefordshire. A Boy's Will (1913) and North of Boston *(1914) were published.* We'd had the usual domestic parleys about this, idle ones, the only kind we Frosts ever engaged in. Elinor, after making that first big resistance—before I married her—to being swept into my good-for-nothing life, accepted everything. First we'd thought of Vancouver as a refuge. But somebody told us it was too expensive. Then I suggested England.

"Yes, let's go over there and sleep under thatch!" cried Elinor. Ever since I found the little book at Dartmouth I'd wanted to visit the land of *The Golden Treasury*. "Let's toss a coin," I proposed. The coin chose England. So we began really to move to sell the Derry farm. . . .

I had no letters of introduction. I knew not one soul in England. But I felt impelled to lose myself among strangers, to write poetry without further scandal to friends or family.[34]

After a tiresome search, Robert found this little cottage we are in now. We have been here just six weeks. It is in the town of Beaconsfield, twenty miles out of London. The rent is higher than we expected it would be, for we were told rents were very cheap here, but it is a dear little cottage of five rooms. It is a low cottage, built of stucco, with vines growing over it, and we have plenty of land with it—a large grassy space in front, and a pretty garden behind, with pear trees, strawberry beds and lots of flowers. We bought enough furniture to get along with for about $125, and shall sell it again when we leave. Our plan is to stay here for a year, and then go over to France for a year, if our courage holds out.[35]

I have never written poetry every day, as you know. It was just every so often that I would weed out this pile or do something to a poem. One evening I found myself sitting on the floor by the fireplace, burning what I could spare. These were poems of youth, written separately, between 1892 and 1912, not in a design to be together.

They were all of a period when I thought I preferred nature to people, quite at the mercy of myself, not always happy. They represented a sort of clinical curve. I put the poems in my pocket, and the next day realized they had a unity, could be a book (*A Boy's Will*).

The poetry itself represented evasiveness, furtiveness. The boy in the poems couldn't be publicly a poet. He was too shy . . . I wrote some prose lines to tie them together. Thirty-some poems. . . .[36]

Then I went down to London to see a man whom I hardly knew—the man who had told me where I could get my little cottage—and see. if he could tell me of some publisher who might buy my verse. He was an ex-policeman. I had no letters of introduction when I went to England.

I asked him if he knew of some small respectable publisher who might buy my poems and not kick me out of the door. He said that no one published poems and that I would myself have to pay to have them printed. I never wanted to do that. Somehow I never liked the idea.

In the conversation this man named David Nutt. Then and there I went over to Nutt's establishment, left the poems, and in two days he wrote me to come in to sign a contract. So you see it was a very accidental beginning.[37]

It was instinct that kept me going in the direction I took, all the time. A sort of feeling told me that I was doing the right thing. I cannot explain it. I had made up my mind not to have my poetry recognized. So, of course, the day my poetry was accepted in England was one of the happiest days of my life.[38]

One of the first [reviews] appeared in *T. P.'s Weekly*, which reviewed Rob's book along with five other new books of poetry. What was said was favorable enough, but the author of the article reviewed the six "in order of merit," placing *A Boy's Will* in fifth place. John [Bartlett], with the indignation of a loyal friend, wrote Frost asking, "Who is this fellow setting himself up as an authority?" The answer was dated "Fourth-of-July, 1913":

> Those initials you quote from T.P.'s belong to a fellow named Buckley, and the explanation of Buckley is this that he has recently issued a book with David Nutt, but at his own expense, whereas in my case David Nutt assumed the risks. *And* those other people Buckley reviewed are his personal friends or friends of his friends or, if not that, simply examples of the kind of wrong horse most fools put their money on. You will be sorry to hear me say so but they are not even craftsmen. . . . To be perfectly frank with you I am one of the most notable craftsmen of my time. That will transpire presently. I am possibly the only person going who works on any but a worn out theory (principle I had better say) of versification. . . .[39]

Lawrance Thompson comments on this period of Frost's life in England. He had inherited some of his father's gambling instincts, and he took additional risks on his talent as a poet. Instead of waiting in Beaconsfield to see how his little book might make out with reviewers, he began a public relations campaign to attract the attention of authors in London who might help to promote the book. He arranged to attend the opening of Harold Monro's Poetry Bookshop, and there made the acquaintance of F. S. Flint, a prominent figure in the early stages of the Imagist movement. It was Flint who told Ezra Pound about Frost, but it was Frost who went to call on Pound as soon as he had the opportunity.

By the time *A Boy's Will* was published, Frost had met and cultivated friendships with several important poets and critics who helped him greatly by reviewing and praising his book. In America the first review to appear was Ezra Pound's in *Poetry* magazine, and much of the biographical information it gave concerning the newly discovered poet of New England had been acquired directly from Frost. But the aesthetic and temperamental differences of the two men quickly resulted in estrangement. . . .[40]

Frost, in a conversation with students at Amherst, from the film A Lover's Quarrel with the World, *described his first encounter with Ezra Pound:* . . . I met him the first time, he said, "I hear you have a book coming out." And I said, "Yes." And he said, "Isn't it out?" and I said, "I don't know; I wouldn't dare to ask the publisher." And he said, "Let's go over and see if we can get one." And he got one, put it in his pocket, and we came away. Then he went back to his room.

And I had this feeling you want to have. I was a little glad that it was out, or something. Very glad. I suppose I walked on air, as they say. I was too old, too old to be *too* excited.

And then, Pound . . . Pound was a novelty to me. I didn't know what kind of a creature he was—and he, ten years younger than I—but he said, "Find something to read," in the bookcase, you know, and I found something to read. And he was behind me reading my book. I hadn't touched it! And he said, "You don't mind our liking this?" I said, "No—go ahead and like it."

That's the way it, career, began. And he seemed to like it. Then presently he said, "You better run along home. I'm going to review this book." Just like that. And I ran along home.[41]

By the time *North of Boston* was published, in May of 1914, he had become so skillfully enterprising as his own promoter that some of the best reviews reflected his careful coaching.[42]

Robert Frost upon his return from England, 1915.

From Little Iddens, where the Frosts moved to be near their poet friends, Elinor Frost wrote to Leona White Harvey a description of their life. We are enjoying a beautiful summer. The weather has been almost perfect since the middle of April, though we have had too many rainy days this last week. I wish I could make you feel what a lovely country this is. When we first came, the meadows were covered with yellow daffodils and the cuckoo had just begun to sing. For nearly two months it sang all day long, but it has already stopped singing. The pastures here are so rich that they are just as green as the mowing and wheat fields, and they are separated by dark green hedges and bordered by huge elms. Great flocks of sheep and herds of cows are everywhere. From a hill about four miles away, one can see the Severn River winding along and the mountains of Wales in the distance. The cottage we are living in is very old—about 350 years old, and all the floors downstairs are brick tiled and the beams show above. We have five rooms and the rent is only fifty dollars a year. . . .

I don't know whether we shall stay here through next winter or not. It will be a little dreary here in winter, I am afraid. At least it will seem so after such a glorious summer as this.[43]

The Frosts returned to the United States in 1915. We grow more and more concerned for our future. The prose I sometimes talk of writing for bread and butter would simply bring me nothing now if I wrote it. I may have to go home soon. The difficulty there is that the expense of getting home would leave me under the necessity of getting a job for a while till I got on my feet again. I should awfully like a quiet job in a small college where I should be allowed to teach something a little new on the technique of writing and where I should have some honor (just a little

25

bit) for what I suppose myself to have done in poetry. Well, but I mustn't dream.[44]

In August 1914, when war broke out, Frost suddenly wanted to get his family and himself back to America. As soon as they could get passage, they all sailed on a small one-cabin-class steamer. When they landed in New York, he had only a few dollars left. They carried their hand luggage across town to the Elevated, took a train to 42nd Street and a 42nd Street trolley across to Grand Central.

On one of the newsstands they passed, Frost's eye was caught by the first issue of the *New Republic* with his name and the title "The Death of the Hired Man" displayed on the cover. He had never heard of the *New Republic;* he had not even heard that Henry Holt and Company were publishing his poems in the United States. He left his family sitting in the station and, following the note about the forthcoming publication of the book, was soon in my [Holt's] office. The *New Republic's* check meant he and his family could get to New Hampshire and start their life again in America.[45]

Frost reflected on the years in New Hampshire and England in a letter to William Stanley Braithwaite, critic for the Boston Evening Transcript.

22 March [1915]

Dear Mr. Braithwaite:

. . . The book [*A Boy's Will*] is an expression of my life for the ten years from eighteen on when I thought I greatly preferred stocks and stones to people. The poems were written as I lived the life quite at the mercy of myself and not always happy. The arrangement in a book came much later when I could

Robert and Elinor Frost: drawing from passport photo.

27

look back on the past with something like under-standing.

I kept farm, so to speak, for nearly ten years, but less as a farmer than as a fugitive from the world that seemed to me to "disallow" me. It was all instinctive, but I can see now that I went away to save myself and fix myself before I measured my strength against all creation. I was never really out of the world for good and all. I liked people even when I believed I detested them. . . .

I say all this biographically to lead up to Book II (*North of Boston*). There came a day about ten years ago when I made the discovery that though sequestered I wasn't living without reference to other people. Right on top of that I made the discovery in doing "The Death of the Hired Man" that I was interested in neighbors for more than merely their tones of speech—and always had been. I remember about when I began to suspect myself of liking their gossip for its own sake. I justified myself by the example of Napoleon as recently I have had to justify myself in seasickness by the example of Nelson.

I like the actuality of gossip, the intimacy of it. Say what you will, effects of actuality and intimacy are the greatest aim an artist can have. The sense of in-timacy gives the thrill of sincerity. A story must al-ways release a meaning more readily to those who read than life itself as it goes ever releases meaning. Meaning is a great consideration. But a story must never seem to be told primarily for meaning. Any-thing, an inspired irrelevancy even to make it sound as if told the way it is chiefly because it happened that way.

. . . In England I saw a good deal of two or three literary circles in London for a year or two and then went down into Gloucestershire and Herefordshire for another year. I never saw *New* England as clearly as when I was in Old England. . . .[46]

Jean Starr Untermeyer remembers asking: "Robert,"
I questioned, "how is it that, though you had those
twenty unrecognized years, years that must have
tested you fiercely, and caused both you and Elinor
much hardship, how is it that I have never heard you
become bitter?" He looked at me in that quizzical way
we all know so well, the lower lip pushed forward a
bit and only the twinkle in the eye at odds with the
gravity of his face.

"Well," he drawled, "with respect to poetry, I have
always felt like a man entrusted to carry a jar of pre-
cious ointment on his head: I didn't want to spill any
of it; then, you know, one can never tell how the race
will turn out till the end; then . . . then I'm a lucky
man; I've always been able to give full measure." [47]

1915–1963: A summary

*Upon Frost's return from England, the upward curve
to critical acceptance, fame, honors, and success had
begun. Holt, Rinehart and Winston became the American publisher he was to remain with for the rest of
his life. Once back in New England, in 1920, Frost
helped to found the Bread Loaf School of English at
Middlebury College. He returned to teaching on the
college level, teaching at different times at Amherst
College, Dartmouth College, Harvard University, and
the University of Michigan, where he served as one
of the first "poets in residence" in the United States.
But the majority of his time teaching in college was
spent at Amherst.*

*During his life, he won four Pulitzer Prizes, the
only person ever to achieve this honor. As more and
more honors accrued, he was recognized by high gov-
ernment officials. In 1952, he was a delegate to the
World Congress of Writers in São Paulo, Brazil; in
1957, he returned to England as an ambassador of good
will, and also to receive honorary degrees from Ox-*

Frost reading "The Gift Outright" at Kennedy's inauguration, 1961.

ford University, Cambridge University, and the National University of Ireland. He was appointed Consultant in Poetry to the Library of Congress in 1958.

His participation in the inauguration ceremonies for President John F. Kennedy was a milestone in his career; it was the first time a poet had been so honored. For the American people it created an unforgettable image of Frost reciting from memory "The Gift Outright" after the glare of the sun prevented him from reading it.

In 1961, he visited Israel, Athens, and London. He was awarded the Congressional Medal at the White House on March 26, 1962, by President Kennedy on the occasion of Frost's eighty-eighth birthday. In August of the same year, he visited the U.S.S.R. on a "good-will mission" for the U.S. Department of State.

Though honors multiplied and his fame increased to great proportions, Frost experienced many personal tragedies. His closest friend, the poet Edward Thomas, was killed in World War I. His sister, Jeanie, became mentally ill and was hospitalized in 1920. In 1934, his daughter Marjorie died after childbirth as a result of septicemia. Marjorie had been a victim of illness throughout her life, but had recovered from tuberculosis to find a brief time of happiness with the young man she married, Willard E. Fraser. A year after her marriage, she died.

The tragedy which nearly defeated Frost was the death of his wife, Elinor, in 1938. Says Louis Untermeyer: It was hard for Robert to maintain his balance after Elinor's death. He sold the Amherst house where he and Elinor had lived; he resigned from the college; he talked recklessly; and, for the first time in his life, the man whose favorite tipple was ginger ale accepted any drink that was offered . . . there was a long black period before he found anything resembling peace.[48]

Frost wrote of his wife: She has been the unspoken half of everything I ever wrote, and both halves of many a thing from My November Guest down to the last stanzas of Two Tramps in Mud Time—as you may have divined. . . .[49]

. . . She could always be present to govern my loneliness without making me feel less alone. It is now running into more than a week longer than I was ever away from her since June 1895. You can see how I might have doubts of myself. I am going to work very hard in May and be on the go with people so as not to try myself solitary too soon.

I suppose love must always deceive. I'm afraid I deceived her a little in pretending for the sake of argument that I didn't think the world was as bad a place as she did. My excuse was that I wanted to keep her

31

a little happy for my own selfish pleasure. It is as if for the sake of argument she had sacrificed her life to give me this terrible answer and really bring me down in sorrow. She needn't have. I knew I never had a leg to stand on, and I should think I had said so in print. . . .[50]

He was later to lose his only son, Carol, through suicide and to see his daughter Irma hospitalized as an invalid. One minister, commenting on Frost's personal tragedies, referred to him as a "Job in our time."

Celebrated as one of the greatest poets America has produced, Robert Frost lived to be eighty-eight years of age. When Frost was in his eighty-seventh year, Louis Untermeyer wrote the following description of him: . . . There is nothing feeble or soft about him, no weakening of posture or power; he is still wide-shouldered, craggy, tough in texture, solid as New Hampshire granite. He is still disillusioned about Progress; distrustful of Science which has taken man deeper and deeper into matter, further into space, and further away from the spirit. He says he will call his last book *The Great Misgiving*.

He continues to think in metaphors, to play with ideas in the old bantering way; he will take no one, including himself, with complete seriousness. "My ironies don't seem to iron out anything." He still believes that the only way to be saved is to save yourself; two of his favorite books are *Robinson Crusoe*, the self-sustaining castaway, and *Walden*, the document of a man who cast himself away to find himself.

He is still against One World, World Federalism, Universal Brotherhood, unity, conformity, the breaking down of barriers in the interest of Oneness; he is unalterably against One Anything. You may quote him to the effect that "Something there is that doesn't love a wall," but you can be sure that he much prefers the opposed quotation that "Good fences make good neighbors." He insists on Nature's divisions and differences; ". . . in art, as in nature, we want all the differences we can get. In society, too. We want people and nations to maintain their differences—even at the risk of trouble, even at the risk of fighting one another." [51]

To the end of his life, he was concerned with poetry. From his deathbed he wrote his last letter to G. R. and Alma Elliott on January 12, 1963. In it he said: We read each other's books and we know what we're thinking about. Metaphor is it and the freshness thereof.[52]

He died on January 23. John Ciardi wrote: And what better mourns a poet than the act of reading him again, so to be stored and restored by him? . . . He was our best.[53]

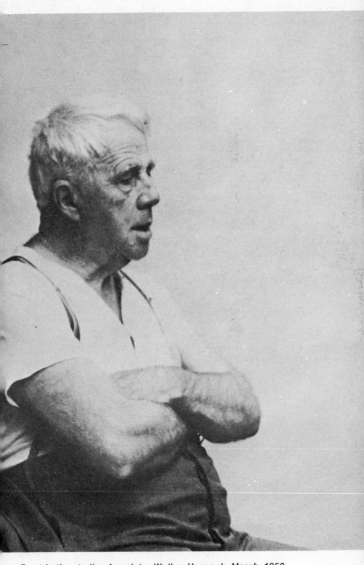

Frost in the studio of sculptor Walker Hancock, March, 1950.

II

Frost: The Poet

My poems—I should suppose everybody's poems—are set to trip the reader head foremost into the boundless. Ever since infancy I have had the habit of leaving my blocks, carts, chairs, and such like ordinaries where people would be pretty sure to fall forward over them in the dark. Forward, you understand, *and* in the dark.[54]

It may seem odd that a poet should compare writing poetry to leaving toys out where people will trip over them. For one thing, one does not ordinarily think of adults indulging in such mischief. For another, too many people think of poetry as a pretty and fanciful use of language—pleasant enough in small doses, but hardly something to pitch its reader headlong into unexpected and frightening experiences. Yet, odd or not, this passage from a letter Frost wrote in 1927 provides a useful clue to understanding his poetry.

In the same letter, he went on to say: "It is my intention we are speaking of—my innate mischievousness." In another letter, written more than fourteen years before, he advised his correspondent: Do not make the mistake of "assuming that my simplicity is that of the untutored child. I am not undesigning."

By his own admission, Frost is mischievous and capable of deception. But why does he want to trip his readers into the boundless dark? To find the answer, we must consider why children also play tricks on adults. Both children and poets want to disturb the life of adults: children, to get attention, and poets, to use this attention to focus the reader's thoughts on reality. Frost's purpose in tripping the reader, then, is to make him think about the realities in life—man's relation to the world around him. In the passage quoted above, Frost is saying that as a poet he falls back on a trick of childhood to achieve this purpose; by putting a harmless toy—a poem—in the reader's way, he trips him into a new experience, perhaps painful, from which the reader may learn something important.

As you read the poems that follow, it will be well to avoid assuming that Frost's "simplicity is that of the untutored child." The nature poem to Frost is just one kind of toy to trip the reader into unexpected ideas on what life is.

All good poetry seems to talk about one thing while really talking about something else. This is because the most important statements about life cannot be understood simply in a sentence. They require investigation for understanding. A good poem, like a full life, may appear simple on the surface, but has many undercurrents of meaning. The investigation of a poem can reveal the proper interpretation of the poet's statement. There is much to be discovered from the poems that follow, and, mainly, it is not about trees and rivers and flowers.

1   Nature and Man

Nature within her inmost self divides
To trouble men with having to take sides.[55]

What are the sides and which side does man choose?
All the poems in this section illustrate this question,
but even from the first, "Come In," you can begin to
guess what the choice will be.

COME IN

As I came to the edge of the woods,
Thrush music—hark!
Now if it was dusk outside,
Inside it was dark.

Too dark in the woods for a bird   5
By sleight of wing
To better its perch for the night,
Though it still could sing.

The last of the light of the sun
That had died in the west   10
Still lived for one song more
In a thrush's breast.

Far in the pillared dark
Thrush music went—
Almost like a call to come in   15
To the dark and lament.

But no, I was out for stars:
I would not come in.
I meant not even if asked,
And I hadn't been.   20

Frost characteristically sets a specific scene in concrete, dramatic terms and then develops it so as to suggest its deeper psychological significance. In "Come In," what is it that first attracts the speaker to the woods? What does he mean by "the pillared dark" in line 13, and why is it so tempting to him?

Had he said just "no" in line 17, there would be no sense of choosing; however, he said "but no," and one feels he may have weakened for a moment and wanted to go in. You can hear his hesitation and choice. If the woods are more than trees to the speaker, then the stars are more than stars. What does he mean by saying he is "out for stars"?

At the end, pretending politeness, the speaker reasserts his common sense, for he admits that no one invited him into the darkness; his own imagination or desire caused him to interpret the bird's song as an invitation. What word in stanza 4 also indicates that nothing was calling him?

After you have finished this section, you might return to "Come In" and see how many meanings and associations the woods and stars have come to have for you. Whenever he could, Frost preferred to stand out in starlight. But he was aware all his life that the forest was always there, threatening to blot out the starlight with darkness.

NEITHER OUT FAR NOR IN DEEP

The people along the sand
All turn and look one way.
They turn their back on the land.
They look at the sea all day.

As long as it takes to pass   5
A ship keeps raising its hull;
The wetter ground like glass
Reflects a standing gull.

The land may vary more;
But wherever the truth may be—   10
The water comes ashore,
And the people look at the sea.

They cannot look out far.
They cannot look in deep.
But when was that ever a bar   15
To any watch they keep?

The people on the beach get only a very simple view of the sea. What is there about the meter and rhyme of this poem to suggest simplicity and almost childish directness?

The details in the second stanza refer to two optical illusions. The curvature of the earth causes the ship's hull to appear to rise, while the gull is reflected in a mirror image. Thus the observer cannot see beyond the near horizon, nor beneath the light-reflecting surface of the water. The land would seem to offer far more variety to his gaze (line 9). Why, then, do the people continue to contemplate the sea? What do they hope to discover, and what quality in men causes them to keep up their watch? Why are people more attracted to the mysterious than to the predictable?

THE OVEN BIRD °

There is a singer everyone has heard,
Loud, a mid-summer and a mid-wood bird,
Who makes the solid tree trunks sound again.
He says that leaves are old and that for flowers
Mid-summer is to spring as one to ten.   5
He says the early petal-fall is past
When pear and cherry bloom went down in
    showers
On sunny days a moment overcast;
And comes that other fall we name the fall.
He says the highway dust is over all.   10
The bird would cease and be as other birds
But that he knows in singing not to sing.
The question that he frames in all but words
Is what to make of a diminished thing.

° A bird which builds a domed
nest

Very few birds sing loudly in mid-summer, but the oven bird's song is so loud that it causes the trees to echo. To the speaker, it seems to sing questions, not celebrations, of the passing of spring and the coming of fall; mid-summer is already a decline, a time when only one flower blooms for every ten that bloomed earlier (lines 4–5).

Like Shakespeare and John Donne, Frost uses such devices as puns and paradoxes to serious intent. The two "falls" in line 9 (which already play on the "petal-fall" of line 6) can be read to imply not only the season, but also: the fall of all leaves and blossoms; the Biblical Fall of Man; declining powers in general; and death itself. What meaning beyond its literal one might "highway dust" have (line 10)? Can you explain the apparent paradox of the singer who "knows in singing not to sing" (line 12)?

Why would Frost be more interested in this "singer" than in the birds that celebrate the spring? Notice that the bird doesn't ask the question in the last line. As with the thrush in "Come In," the words are in the listener, the poet, and it is he who reads this meaning into the song. What is the "diminished thing," and how would you answer the question posed?

DESIGN

I found a dimpled spider, fat and white,
On a white heal-all,° holding up a moth
Like a white piece of rigid satin cloth—
Assorted characters of death and blight
Mixed ready to begin the morning right,   5
Like the ingredients of a witches' broth—
A snow-drop spider, a flower like a froth,
And dead wings carried like a paper kite.

What had that flower to do with being white,
The wayside blue and innocent heal-all?   10
What brought the kindred spider to that
    height,
Then steered the white moth thither in the
    night?
What but design of darkness to appall?—
If design govern in a thing so small.

° Usually, a blue wild flower
thought to have medicinal
qualities

Frost achieves utter horror in this poem, which many consider his most terrifying work, by juxtaposing pleasant images with disgusting ones: the fat spider is "dimpled" and "white" like a baby; "dead wings" become a "paper kite"; "death and blight" are cheerfully "mixed ready to begin the morning right," as in an ad for breakfast food. An air of abnormality pervades the entire poem. The flower, ironically called the "heal-all," is usually blue, but this is a mutant. The spider is at a height where it would not normally be found. Moths are ordinarily attracted by light, but this one has been "steered" to its death in the night. And all the "characters of death" share the same ghastly whiteness.

Can we escape the conclusion that a dark design in nature plotted against the moth? The last line may not offer the ray of light its tone suggests. What would be better—that darkness terrorize by design, or that all the little evils in the world operate without design?

Consider also the game Frost plays with the reader by calling this sonnet "Design." A sonnet is a very small, yet intricately designed, poetic form of 14 lines; yet the speaker asks at the end if design really governs in very small things. Work out the poem's rhyme scheme, and then decide what answer he wants you to give.

You might find it interesting to compare the imagery and ideas of this poem with the following two stanzas of William Blake's "The Tiger."

> Tiger! Tiger! burning bright
> In the forests of the night,
> What immortal hand or eye,
> Could frame thy fearful symmetry?
>
> .   .   .
>
> When the stars threw down their spears,
> And watered heaven with their tears,
> Did he smile his work to see?
> Did he who made the Lamb make thee?

THE LOVELY SHALL BE CHOOSERS

The Voice said, 'Hurl her down!'

The Voices, 'How far down?'

'Seven levels of the world.'

'How much time have we?'

'Take twenty years.   5
She *would* refuse love safe with wealth and
      honor!
The lovely shall be choosers, shall they?
Then let them choose!'

'Then we shall let her choose?'

'Yes, let her choose.   10
Take up the task beyond her choosing.'

Invisible hands crowded on her shoulder
In readiness to weigh upon her.
But she stood straight still,
In broad round ear-rings, gold and jet with
      pearls   15
And broad round suchlike brooch,
Her cheeks high colored,
Proud and the pride of friends.

The Voice asked, 'You can let her choose?'

'Yes, we can let her and still triumph.'   20

'Do it by joys, and leave her always blameless.
Be her first joy her wedding,
That though a wedding,
Is yet—well something they know, he and she.
And after that her next joy   25

That though she grieves, her grief is secret:
Those friends know nothing of her grief to
    make it shameful.
Her third joy that though now they cannot help
    but know,
They move in pleasure too far off
To think much or much care.   30
Give her a child at either knee for fourth joy
To tell once and once only, for them never to
    forget,
How once she walked in brightness,
And make them see it in the winter firelight.
But give her friends for then she dare not tell   35
For their foregone incredulousness.
And be her next joy this:
Her never having deigned to tell them.
Make her among the humblest even
Seem to them less than they are.   40
Hopeless of being known for what she has been,
Failing of being loved for what she is,
Give her the comfort for her sixth of knowing
She fails from strangeness to a way of life
She came to from too high too late to learn.   45
Then send some *one* with eyes to see
And wonder at her where she is,
And words to wonder in her hearing how she
    came there,
But without time to linger for her story.
Be her last joy her heart's going out to this one   50
So that she almost speaks.
You know them—seven in all.'

'Trust us,' the Voices said.

Can any of us live life on our own terms, or does some "design of darkness" in nature entrap even those who believe themselves free? In this poem, the dark force is represented by "the Voice" and the assistant "Voices." They work with infinite patience—over a span of twenty years —and with infinite subtlety. A beautiful and proud young woman is to be brought low, but not, as we might expect, by a series of chance misfortunes, nor even by her own error and involvement in evil. She will be free to choose the roads to travel in her life, but with terrible irony, each choice will only add to her suffering and humiliation.

Her first choice is the rejection of a suitor who would give her "love safe with wealth and honor" in favor of a less conventional man. But the marriage is marred by some secret failure (line 24)—Frost does not tell us exactly what. Explain in detail the woman's "joys" from this point on. How do her most noble characteristics contribute to her isolation and unhappiness? Do you think Frost meant to suggest that she would have been happy if she had chosen the "safer" husband originally? Where does "the road not taken" lead?

Frost himself was quoted by one interviewer as saying: "It's a poem—well [he evaded], it has a lot to do with women. [He hesitated.] It's about my mother." [56]

ACQUAINTED WITH THE NIGHT

I have been one acquainted with the night.
I have walked out in rain—and back in rain.
I have outwalked the furthest city light.

I have looked down the saddest city lane.
I have passed by the watchman on his beat   5
And dropped my eyes, unwilling to explain.

I have stood still and stopped the sound of feet
When far away an interrupted cry
Came over houses from another street,

But not to call me back or say good-by;   10
And further still at an unearthly height,
One luminary clock against the sky

Proclaimed the time was neither wrong nor
    right.
I have been one acquainted with the night.

This poem is concerned not only with the literal night through which the speaker walks, but also with a mental state—something akin to the religious experience known as "the dark night of the soul." Here, as in poems like "Come In," "Design," "Once by the Pacific," "The Draft Horse," and "Stopping by Woods," Frost is both attracted and repelled by darkness. Within the framework of conventional versification, Frost expresses a totally modern feeling of alienation and estrangement. Man is out of contact with his fellow men in a universe which totally ignores him.

Notice how each detail adds to the feeling of complete absence of communication. What do you think the speaker is "unwilling to explain" in line 6? Lines 7–10 hint that he might like to be called back or spoken to. What might this "interrupted cry" be, if not a call to him? In line 13, what is the time "neither wrong nor right" for?

It is unusual to find a city setting in a poem by Frost. Why do you think he chose one for "Acquainted with the Night"?

DESERT PLACES

Snow falling and night falling fast, oh, fast
In a field I looked into going past,
And the ground almost covered smooth in
 snow,
But a few weeds and stubble showing last.

The woods around it have it—it is theirs.   5
All animals are smothered in their lairs.
I am too absent-spirited to count;
The loneliness includes me unawares.

And lonely as it is that loneliness
Will be more lonely ere it will be less—   10
A blanker whiteness of benighted snow
With no expression, nothing to express.

They cannot scare me with their empty spaces
Between stars—on stars where no human race
 is.
I have it in me so much nearer home   15
To scare myself with my own desert places.

Once again Frost combines blank whiteness (as in "Design") with the darkness of night to convey a mood of total isolation. As the images of nature's indifference and barren coldness pile up, the speaker's own "absent-spirited" state (line 7) is reflected in the scene. But he denies any feeling of harmony or communication with nature, even in loneliness. The surrounding woods no longer attract him as they did in "Come In"; Frost uses them to suggest the elemental chaos which stands ready to engulf us when we stop making form, whether it be ploughed land or poetry. Soon the field itself will be a smooth, formless void, "with no expression, nothing to express" (line 12). How many different meanings can "benighted" have in line 11?

When he wrote lines 13–14, Frost may have been thinking of modern astronomers with their reports of the fantastic dimensions of interstellar space. Why does Frost insist on staying "nearer home"? Notice also that stanza 3 uses very formal poetic diction: "ere," "benighted"; while stanza 4 has the childish phrase "scare myself" and the humorous double rhyme "spaces—race is." Why is there this contrast between stanzas?

ONCE BY THE PACIFIC

The shattered water made a misty din.
Great waves looked over others coming in,
And thought of doing something to the shore
That water never did to land before.
The clouds were low and hairy in the skies,   5
Like locks blown forward in the gleam of eyes.
You could not tell, and yet it looked as if
The shore was lucky in being backed by cliff,
The cliff in being backed by continent;
It looked as if a night of dark intent   10
Was coming, and not only a night, an age.
Someone had better be prepared for rage.
There would be more than ocean-water broken
Before God's last *Put out the Light* was spoken.

There is more than waves battering the continent in this
early poem. What details of Frost's description suggest a
malicious and frightening personal enemy?

In the story of the Creation in Genesis, God's first words
are "Let there be light." He later goes on to separate the
waters from the dry land. What is the significance of
Frost's play on God's words in the last line?

At this point you might stop to consider the range of
attitudes towards nature which you have met in Frost's
poems so far. Is nature the almost wise teacher of "Come
In" and "The Oven Bird," or the lonely indifference of
"Acquainted with the Night" and "Desert Places," or the
malicious enemy of this poem and "The Draft Horse,"
which follows?

FIRE AND ICE

Some say the world will end in fire,
Some say in ice.
From what I've tasted of desire
I hold with those who favor fire.
But if it had to perish twice,   5
I think I know enough of hate
To say that for destruction ice
Is also great
And would suffice.

In "Fire and Ice" Frost transforms a genuine scientific
controversy over the end of the world into a personal, psychological question. Notice the characteristic "objectivity"
of the ending, and the speaker's use of understatement in
lines 7–9. Why do you think he chooses "suffice" to express this destruction rather than a stronger word like "ex-
terminate" or "annihilate"?

THE DRAFT HORSE °

With a lantern that wouldn't burn
In too frail a buggy we drove
Behind too heavy a horse
Through a pitch-dark limitless grove.

And a man came out of the trees   5
And took our horse by the head
And reaching back to his ribs
Deliberately stabbed him dead.

The ponderous beast went down
With a crack of a broken shaft.   10
And the night drew through the trees
In one long invidious * draft.

The most unquestioning pair
That ever accepted fate
And the least disposed to ascribe   15
Any more than we had to to hate,

We assumed that the man himself
Or someone he had to obey
Wanted us to get down
And walk the rest of the way.   20

° A heavy, powerful farm horse
* Hateful

Frost once said in a letter: "Something hates us and likes to spoil our fair beginnings." [57] This theme became more and more frequent in the last quarter of his life, and he seemed increasingly to see nature as a force actively hindering man's journey. "The Draft Horse" was published in his last volume, *In the Clearing*. Assuming that the buggy ride through the night-black forest is symbolic, how would you interpret the following details: the "lantern that wouldn't burn," the "too heavy a horse," "too frail a buggy," and the man who stabs?

Is this a chance misfortune, or part of a divinely ordained plan? There is a strong suggestion that someone else sent the man. Who? Notice that whoever it was seems to be working by design to allow the couple to get away —even if it is for a much more difficult trip! Take into account also that the couple does not fight back nor sob in despair. The key word is "accept" (line 14). They are even unwilling to think it was hatred of them that caused the man to stab their horse (lines 15–16). They do not trouble themselves over why such a disaster should befall them, but accept it as if they had expected something like this to happen. Is this because of fear? Or reasonableness? Or courage? Or experience?

The poems in the next section explore more fully this question of man's response to his fate.

2 Courage

The Act of Living

You've got to be brave and you've got to be bold. Brave enough to take your chance on your own discriminations—what's right and what's wrong, what's good and what's bad.[58]

Many of the poems presented so far dealt with what man finds dark and frightening in nature or in himself. What a person does—how he acts—when he is frightened tells a great deal about his character. Frost believed that man should face up to the indifference and hostility of nature, accept the disturbing qualities within himself, and go about his daily affairs with courage. As the following group of poems suggests, for Frost courage is not fighting back; it is the power to endure.

'OUT, OUT—'

The buzz saw snarled and rattled in the yard
And made dust and dropped stove-length sticks
   of wood,
Sweet-scented stuff when the breeze drew across it.
And from there those that lifted eyes could count
Five mountain ranges one behind the other   5
Under the sunset far into Vermont.
And the saw snarled and rattled, snarled and
   rattled,
As it ran light, or had to bear a load.
And nothing happened: day was all but done.
Call it a day, I wish they might have said   10
To please the boy by giving him the half hour
That a boy counts so much when saved from
   work.
His sister stood beside them in her apron
To tell them 'Supper.' At the word, the saw,
As if to prove saws knew what supper meant,   15
Leaped out at the boy's hand, or seemed to leap—
He must have given the hand. However it was,
Neither refused the meeting. But the hand!
The boy's first outcry was a rueful laugh,
As he swung toward them holding up the hand   20
Half in appeal, but half as if to keep
The life from spilling. Then the boy saw all—
Since he was old enough to know, big boy
Doing a man's work, though a child at heart—
He saw all spoiled. 'Don't let him cut my hand
   off—   25
The doctor, when he comes. Don't let him,
   sister!'
So. But the hand was gone already.
The doctor put him in the dark of ether.
He lay and puffed his lips out with his breath.

And then—the watcher at his pulse took fright. ^{30}
No one believed. They listened at his heart.
Little—less—nothing!—and that ended it.
No more to build on there. And they, since they
Were not the one dead, turned to their affairs.

Frost once said that he never chose this poem for a poetry reading because it was too horrible. It is based on a newspaper article about an incident in his neighborhood, and it illustrates probably better than any other poem in this book Frost's feeling that "everything written is as good as it is dramatic."

Notice particularly the way Frost sets the scene in the first nine lines, creating the time, place, sound, smell, and the reality of the work which the boy is sharing. Lines 4–6, however, are not merely stage setting. They are the sinister hint of what would cause one using a buzz saw to lift his eyes from his hand at the saw for a moment.

Lines 1 and 7 are onomatopoeic (they contain words which sound like the thing they are describing). Can you find other examples of onomatopoeia in the poem?

Frost also makes extensive use of understatement in this poem. Reread lines 10–12, 15–18, 25 (the first half), and 32–34. Do you think that understatement, as seen in those lines, is an appropriate way to express so violent a death?

The tone of the last two lines has aroused particular debate. The boy's death, and the helplessness of those around him to prevent it, might have caused them to despair. Despair is certainly the tone of the passage from *Macbeth*, V, v, from which Frost took the title of his poem:

> Out, out, brief candle!
> Life's but a walking shadow, a poor player
> That struts and frets his hour upon the stage
> And then is heard no more.

But instead of pouring out their grief, the boy's family simply take up their work again. Does Frost wish us to condemn the living or respect them for turning to their affairs in the face of tragedy? Is it courage or indifference that makes the living return to their affairs?

RELUCTANCE

Out through the fields and the woods
    And over the walls I have wended;
I have climbed the hills of view
    And looked at the world, and descended;
I have come by the highway home,   5
    And lo, it is ended.

The leaves are all dead on the ground,
    Save those that the oak is keeping
To ravel ° them one by one
    And let them go scraping and creeping   10
Out over the crusted snow,
    When others are sleeping.

And the dead leaves lie huddled and still,
    No longer blown hither and thither;
The last lone aster is gone;   15
    The flowers of the witch-hazel wither;
The heart is still aching to seek,
    But the feet question 'Whither?'

Ah, when to the heart of man
    Was it ever less than a treason   20
To go with the drift of things,
    To yield with a grace to reason,
And bow and accept the end
    Of a love or a season?

° Disentangle

This poem was probably written in the 1890's. Notice Frost's use of words like "lo," "wended," and "hither and thither." Would you expect to find these in modern poetry? Compare the diction with that of " 'Out, Out—,' " which was written much later.

The mood of "Reluctance" also contrasts with Frost's celebration of acceptance in " 'Out, Out—.' " The inevitable "drift of things," the demands of "reason," and the everyday common sense spoken for by the feet (line 18) are all clear enough. But the heart never gives up its desire to fight; for it, surrender to the inevitable is "treason." What do you think the heart is "still aching to seek" in line 17? Does the speaker imply that if you, with courage, do not "accept the end," you will therefore win? Or are there occasions when you win without winning? Can you find other examples in Frost's poetry of this conflict between common sense and what might be called the heart's reasons?

Dylan Thomas pleaded in a similar vein:

> Do not go gentle into that good night
> Rage, rage against the dying of the light.[59]

Why shouldn't you bow to the inevitable? Do you think there are times when you should?

TO EARTHWARD

Love at the lips was touch
As sweet as I could bear;
And once that seemed too much;
I lived on air

That crossed me from sweet things   5
The flow of—was it musk °
From hidden grapevine springs
Down hill at dusk?

I had the swirl and ache
From sprays of honeysuckle   10
That when they're gathered shake
Dew on the knuckle.

I craved strong sweets, but those
Seemed strong when I was young;
The petal of the rose   15
It was that stung.

Now no joy but lacks salt
That is not dashed with pain
And weariness and fault;
I crave the stain   20

Of tears, the aftermark
Of almost too much love,
The sweet of bitter bark
And burning clove.

When stiff and sore and scarred   25
I take away my hand
From leaning on it hard
In grass and sand,

° A heavy scent

The hurt is not enough:
I long for weight and strength   30
To feel the earth as rough
To all my length.

"To Earthward" is Frost's record of the burden of experience, the cost of the act of living. Trace in detail the
contrasting images that express the difference between the
passions in youth and age. Is the descent "to earthward"
entirely a process of diminution and loss? Some critics
have felt that the last stanza hints at a death wish. Do you
agree?

THE ROAD NOT TAKEN

Two roads diverged in a yellow wood,
And sorry I could not travel both
And be one traveler, long I stood
And looked down one as far as I could
To where it bent in the undergrowth;   5

Then took the other, as just as fair,
And having perhaps the better claim,
Because it was grassy and wanted wear;
Though as for that the passing there
Had worn them really about the same,   10

And both that morning equally lay
In leaves no step had trodden black.
Oh, I kept the first for another day!
Yet knowing how way leads on to way,
I doubted if I should ever come back.   15

I shall be telling this with a sigh
Somewhere ages and ages hence:
Two roads diverged in a wood, and I—
I took the one less traveled by,
And that has made all the difference.   20

If we read this poem focusing on lines 7–8 and 19, Frost seems to be saying that, faced with a choice between two roads, the speaker chose the less used, less popular, more adventurous one. And this choice has determined his entire future. Thus the diverging roads become a simple and graphic metaphor for the fact that each of us is what we are as a result of having chosen either a conventional or unconventional way through life.

There is a difficulty, however. Lines 9–12 suggest that, as a matter of fact, there is no real, objective evidence that one road is indeed "less traveled by." This second reading complicates the meaning of the poem and makes the speaker's position far more precarious. Since he has no rational basis for choice, he is thrown back on whim or impulsive desire to "decide" which is the less used road. He must choose his direction in life on little more than a hunch. Yet he must take full responsibility for the consequences.

How does the act of making a choice when the alternatives are about the same take courage? Looking at the last stanza, do you think the speaker is regretful? Triumphant? Satisfied? Bitter? The speaker doesn't tell us in the last line exactly what difference has been made by his choice. What differences can you imagine he means here?

Perhaps this poem reflects the same frustrating conflict which Frost explores in his poems of man's relation to nature. "Acquainted with the Night" and "Desert Places," for example, emphasize that man is totally isolated and is given no hints by an indifferent nature for charting his course in an alien world. "The Draft Horse," on the other hand, portrays nature as making it quite clear which road she wishes man to travel. It may be that the reader's confusion about the traveled quality of the roads represents for Frost nature's maddening trick of giving so much evidence which is no evidence at all.

Retreat for Strength

The most exciting movement in nature is not progress,
advance, but expansion and contraction, the opening
and shutting of the eye, the hand, the heart, the mind.
. . . We throw our arms wide with a gesture of religion to the universe; we close them around a person.
We explore and adventure for awhile and then draw
in to consolidate our gains.[60]

Adventure and retreat are the two parts of man's
courage. The drawing back is as important as the mov-
ing in. This idea occurred to Frost with increasing
frequency as he grew older, although it had always
been in his poetry and in his life: the need for physical,
moral, and spiritual refreshment through leaving the
active world for a time.

BIRCHES

When I see birches bend to left and right
Across the lines of straighter darker trees,
I like to think some boy's been swinging them.
But swinging doesn't bend them down to stay
As ice-storms do. Often you must have seen
them   5
Loaded with ice a sunny winter morning
After a rain. They click upon themselves
As the breeze rises, and turn many-colored
As the stir cracks and crazes their enamel.
Soon the sun's warmth makes them shed crystal
shells   10

76

Shattering and avalanching on the snow-crust—
Such heaps of broken glass to sweep away
You'd think the inner dome of heaven had fallen.
They are dragged to the withered bracken by the
load,
And they seem not to break; though once they
are bowed 15
So low for long, they never right themselves:
You may see their trunks arching in the woods
Years afterwards, trailing their leaves on the
ground
Like girls on hands and knees that throw their
hair
Before them over their heads to dry in the sun. 20
But I was going to say when Truth broke in
With all her matter-of-fact about the ice-storm
I should prefer to have some boy bend them
As he went out and in to fetch the cows—
Some boy too far from town to learn baseball, 25
Whose only play was what he found himself,
Summer or winter, and could play alone.
One by one he subdued his father's trees
By riding them down over and over again
Until he took the stiffness out of them, 30
And not one but hung limp, not one was left
For him to conquer. He learned all there was
To learn about not launching out too soon
And so not carrying the tree away
Clear to the ground. He always kept his poise 35
To the top branches, climbing carefully
With the same pains you use to fill a cup
Up to the brim, and even above the brim.
Then he flung outward, feet first, with a swish,
Kicking his way down through the air to the
ground. 40

So was I once myself a swinger of birches.
And so I dream of going back to be.
It's when I'm weary of considerations,
And life is too much like a pathless wood
Where your face burns and tickles with the
    cobwebs   45
Broken across it, and one eye is weeping
From a twig's having lashed across it open.
I'd like to get away from earth awhile
And then come back to it and begin over.
May no fate willfully misunderstand me   50
And half grant what I wish and snatch me away
Not to return. Earth's the right place for love:
I don't know where it's likely to go better.
I'd like to go by climbing a birch tree,
And climb black branches up a snow-white
    trunk   55
Toward heaven, till the tree could bear no more,
But dipped its top and set me down again.
That would be good both going and coming
    back.
One could do worse than be a swinger of birches.

Frost once said: "'Birches' is two fragments soldered together so long ago I have forgotten where the joint is." [61] One likely place may be around line 21, where the speaker turns from the literal "Truth" (with a capital T) about birches bent by ice storms, to his own memory or fantasy about birch-swinging. Line 3 also indicates that no one is actually swinging the birches. Does such a removal from physical fact make the image stronger or weaker?

Lines 41–49 suggest why the speaker is so imaginatively drawn to his boyhood pastime. He has gone forward to "explore and adventure for awhile," immersing himself in all the complexities and difficulties of experience. Now he needs to "draw in to consolidate [his] gains," to get away from earth for the time being. Birch-swinging is the symbol of the retreat he craves. Why is "considerations" used in line 43 instead of "troubles," "worries," or "problems"? Is it the big or little things in life that he is weary of? Can you imagine what some of them might be?

Looking back at lines 4–20, do you think the point of the poem is disturbed or helped by the "Truth" that some birches (and people?) once bowed to earth never leave it again?

The opposite possibility is suggested in lines 48–53. Robert Frost recognizes the danger of retreat. It may become permanent, thus akin to death. Therefore he prays (line 50) that the Fate which has acted so perversely towards man in his other poems, will not intentionally misunderstand the speaker in "Birches" and grant him half his wish —the retreat part—without granting the return to earth. He desires with all the weariness and experience in his bones to climb towards Heaven, but he hopes that Fate will act like a birch tree (lines 56–57), and that when he gets far enough away from pain and tribulation, he will gracefully and gently be brought back down to earth again. Then his life can be a rhythmic repetition of expansion and contraction, going up and coming down, advancing and retreating.

What, in particular, makes him wish to return always to earth?

In winter in the woods alone
Against the trees I go.
I mark a maple for my own
And lay the maple low.

At four o'clock I shoulder axe
And in the afterglow
I link a line of shadowy tracks
Across the tinted snow.

I see for Nature no defeat
In one tree's overthrow
Or for myself in my retreat
For yet another blow.

All life's actions, suggests Frost, are composed of a rhythm of going forward and pulling back. What details in the poem reflect this rhythm in nature? How does Frost suggest that a woodsman, chopping trees in the forest, must participate in the same rhythm to succeed?

Frost was proud of the continuing rhyme scheme and called it "quite a feat." [62] Specifically, what in the rhyme scheme was he referring to? Do you think it contributes anything to the meaning of the poem?

A professor once accused Frost of choosing the word "retreat" in line 11 simply because it rhymes with "defeat." But Frost, with some annoyance, replied:

> We retreat; we don't escape. That's a word I loathe, you know, "escape." But "retreat" is a sort of characteristic word to me, that you retreat for strength. Church touches that, you know. They're not brought up in the right religion if they don't know what retreat is. You don't escape, you withdraw with God. With sleep.[63]

Frost thus links his idea of retreat with the spiritual discipline of orthodox religion. It is also very close to what the physiologist knows: that without sleep there can be no wakefulness. As he uses the word in this poem, it has military overtones as well. Considering what you have learned about Frost's struggle with nature, do you agree that "retreat" is a more appropriate word than "escape" or "give up"?

AWAY!

Now I out walking
The world desert;
And my shoe and my stocking
Do me no hurt.

I leave behind   5
Good friends in town.
Let them get well-wined
And go lie down.

Don't think I leave
For the outer dark   10
Like Adam and Eve
Put out of the Park.

Forget the myth.
There is no one I
Am put out with   15
Or put out by.

Unless I'm wrong
I but obey
The urge of a song:
I'm—bound—away!   20

And I may return
If dissatisfied
With what I learn
From having died.

In this late poem the speaker has apparently relaxed in his battle with his environment and feels free to choose his destiny on "the urge of a song." The eternal movement of expansion and contraction, retreat and return, still applies, however. Even where death, the ultimate retreat, is concerned, Frost insists on a round-trip ticket. Of course it is merely whimsy to think one can return from death if one doesn't like it. What else, then, might the speaker mean by the last stanza?

3   Labor's Fact

The Sweetest Dream

You know, I've often said that every poem solves
something for me in life. I go so far as to say that every
poem is a momentary stay against the confusion of the
world.[64]

Every man must create his own "momentary stay"
against confusion. Frost believed that this could be
done and is done by a man's work. The indifference of
nature and man's own "desert places" are best met by
the vitality and integrity of labor's fact.

MOWING

There was never a sound beside the wood but
  one,
And that was my long scythe whispering to the
  ground.
What was it it whispered? I knew not well
  myself;
Perhaps it was something about the heat of the
  sun,
Something, perhaps, about the lack of sound—   5
And that was why it whispered and did not speak.
It was no dream of the gift of idle hours,
Or easy gold at the hand of fay ° or elf:
Anything more than the truth would have seemed
  too weak
To the earnest love that laid the swale * in rows,   10
Not without feeble-pointed spikes of flowers
(Pale orchises), and scared a bright green snake.
The fact is the sweetest dream that labor knows.
My long scythe whispered and left the hay to
  make.

° Fairy
* A piece of meadow

Frost regarded "Mowing" as one of his finest poetic achievements: "In 'Mowing,' for instance, I come so near what I long to get that I almost despair of coming nearer." [65] The work of mowing itself embodies the rhythmic advance and retreat pattern which we have seen is essential to Frost. And, as the following quotation shows, making hay and writing poetry were not far apart in his imagination; he wielded scythe and fountain pen with equal love:

> . . . Two or three of my favorite things, I suppose, are the scythe, the hay fork, and fountain pen, see, the baseball bat, and so on. Two of them are just like that, that scythe. I was good with the mowing, the hand mowing. I wish I had a chance to show you. See, I knew a man who could take a scythe, a long, slender scythe, you know, take a lawn and cut it just the same as a lawnmower. Lovely motion, lovely sweep. Beautiful mowing.[66]

This irregularly rhymed sonnet comes closer to defining Frost's approach to poetry than any other poem in this book. Lines 9 and 10 could be a motto for his unadorned, simply stated style, and for the care with which his "rows" are wrought. Since Frost cannot know all truth, what "truth" does his poetry convey? Is he longing or scornful when he compares his heavy labor with the "dream of the gift of idle hours," and "easy gold at the hand of fay or elf" (lines 7–8)? Is the speaker being ironic when he says in line 13 that the fact is a "dream" to labor? Or should the emphasis be on "sweetest" because the other kind of dream (daydream) must go sour?

Frost restates his theme concisely when he ends the poem with "to make." What we make or create is, in some sense, the only fact or reality of which we can be sure. And if we take the word "poet" back to its origins, we find that the Greek root of *poiētēs* means simply "to make."

TWO TRAMPS IN MUD TIME

Out of the mud two strangers came
And caught me splitting wood in the yard.
And one of them put me off my aim
By hailing cheerily 'Hit them hard!'
I knew pretty well why he dropped behind   5
And let the other go on a way.
I knew pretty well what he had in mind:
He wanted to take my job for pay.

Good blocks of oak it was I split,
As large around as the chopping block;   10
And every piece I squarely hit
Fell splinterless as a cloven rock.
The blows that a life of self-control
Spares to strike for the common good
That day, giving a loose to my soul,   15
I spent on the unimportant wood.

The sun was warm but the wind was chill.
You know how it is with an April day
When the sun is out and the wind is still,
You're one month on in the middle of May.   20
But if you so much as dare to speak,
A cloud comes over the sunlit arch,
A wind comes off a frozen peak,
And you're two months back in the middle of
    March.

A bluebird comes tenderly up to alight   25
And turns to the wind to unruffle a plume
His song so pitched as not to excite
A single flower as yet to bloom.

It is snowing a flake: and he half knew
Winter was only playing possum. 30
Except in color he isn't blue,
But he wouldn't advise a thing to blossom.

The water for which we may have to look
In summertime with a witching-wand,°
In every wheelrut's now a brook,   35
In every print of a hoof a pond.
Be glad of water, but don't forget
The lurking frost in the earth beneath
That will steal forth after the sun is set
And show on the water its crystal teeth.   40

The time when most I loved my task
These two must make me love it more
By coming with what they came to ask.
You'd think I never had felt before
The weight of an ax-head poised aloft,   45
The grip on earth of outspread feet.
The life of muscles rocking soft
And smooth and moist in vernal heat.

Out of the woods two hulking tramps
(From sleeping God knows where last night,   50
But not long since in the lumber camps).
They thought all chopping was theirs of right
Men of the woods and lumberjacks,
They judged me by their appropriate tool.
Except as a fellow handled an ax,   55
They had no way of knowing a fool.

° A hand-held branch that some
farmers think indicates under-
ground water

Nothing on either side was said.
They knew they had but to stay their stay
And all their logic would fill my head:
As that I had no right to play   60
With what was another man's work for gain.
My right might be love but theirs was need.
And where the two exist in twain
Theirs was the better right—agreed.

But yield who will to their separation,   65
My object in living is to unite
My avocation and my vocation
As my two eyes make one in sight.
Only where love and need are one,
And the work is play for mortal stakes,   70
Is the deed ever really done
For Heaven and the future's sakes.

The speaker pits himself against the average views of society—he represents the poet's, or lover's, way of looking at life. To him, the hard labor of chopping wood is sweet because of the deep personal satisfaction with which it is done. He loves the season of the year, the material on which he works (lines 9–12), the feel of the ax and the play of his muscles (lines 44–48), and he is even aware that his work is satisfying his soul, though it is on "unimportant wood" (lines 13–16). It is the fact of a job done with satisfaction and even love that makes it sweet. This is what Frost also was saying in "Mowing" and "The Death of the Hired Man."

The two tramps who come hulking out of the woods represent the average view of work. They judge it by the worth of the product in the marketplace, and by how much it will earn them. They see other men not as whole human beings, but simply as extensions of the tools they use in their work (lines 54–56). They themselves are homeless, without roots anywhere. And they need work to stay alive.

The speaker admits in lines 62–64 that when love and need conflict, need has the better right. Logic and worldly common sense are on the side of the tramps. Can you explain in your own words why, then, he doesn't allow the tramps to chop the wood? Does he reject the demands of need altogether?

In good poetry, every detail works towards the main point. Why does the speaker take three stanzas to describe the unstable balance of "an April day"? What do you think the tramps would say about the weather?

THE DEATH OF THE HIRED MAN

Mary sat musing on the lamp-flame at the table
Waiting for Warren. When she heard his step,
She ran on tip-toe down the darkened passage
To meet him in the doorway with the news
And put him on his guard. 'Silas is back.'   5
She pushed him outward with her through the
    door
And shut it after her. 'Be kind,' she said.
She took the market things from Warren's arms
And set them on the porch, then drew him down
To sit beside her on the wooden steps.   10

'When was I ever anything but kind to him?
But I'll not have the fellow back,' he said.
'I told him so last haying, didn't I?
If he left then, I said, that ended it.
What good is he? Who else will harbor him   15
At his age for the little he can do?
What help he is there's no depending on.
Off he goes always when I need him most.
He thinks he ought to earn a little pay,
Enough at least to buy tobacco with,   20
So he won't have to beg and be beholden.
"All right," I say, "I can't afford to pay
Any fixed wages, though I wish I could."
"Someone else can." "Then someone else will
    have to."
I shouldn't mind his bettering himself   25
If that was what it was. You can be certain,
When he begins like that, there's someone at him
Trying to coax him off with pocket-money,—
In haying time, when any help is scarce.
In winter he comes back to us. I'm done.'   30

'Sh! not so loud: he'll hear you,' Mary said.

'I want him to: he'll have to soon or late.'

'He's worn out. He's asleep beside the stove.
When I came up from Rowe's I found him here,
Huddled against the barn-door fast asleep,   35
A miserable sight, and frightening, too—
You needn't smile—I didn't recognize him—
I wasn't looking for him—and he's changed.
Wait till you see.'

                    'Where did you say he'd been?'

'He didn't say. I dragged him to the house,   40
And gave him tea and tried to make him smoke.
I tried to make him talk about his travels.
Nothing would do: he just kept nodding off.'

'What did he say? Did he say anything?'

'But little.'

          'Anything? Mary, confess   45
He said he'd come to ditch the meadow for me.'

'Warren!'

          'But did he? I just want to know.'

'Of course he did. What would you have him
    say?
Surely you wouldn't grudge the poor old man
Some humble way to save his self-respect.   50
He added, if you really care to know,
He meant to clear the upper pasture, too.
That sounds like something you have heard
    before?
Warren, I wish you could have heard the way
He jumbled everything. I stopped to look   55
Two or three times—he made me feel so queer—

To see if he was talking in his sleep.
He ran on Harold Wilson—you remember—
The boy you had in haying four years since.
He's finished school, and teaching in his college.   60
Silas declares you'll have to get him back.
He says they two will make a team for work:
Between them they will lay this farm as smooth!
The way he mixed that in with other things.
He thinks young Wilson a likely lad, though daft   65
On education—you know how they fought
All through July under the blazing sun,
Silas up on the cart to build the load,
Harold along beside to pitch it on.'

'Yes, I took care to keep well out of earshot.'   70

'Well, those days trouble Silas like a dream.
You wouldn't think they would. How some
    things linger!
Harold's young college boy's assurance piqued
    him.
After so many years he still keeps finding
Good arguments he sees he might have used.   75
I sympathize. I know just how it feels
To think of the right thing to say too late.
Harold's associated in his mind with Latin.
He asked me what I thought of Harold's saying
He studied Latin like the violin   80
Because he liked it—that an argument!
He said he couldn't make the boy believe
He could find water with a hazel prong—
Which showed how much good school had ever
    done him.
He wanted to go over that. But most of all   85
He thinks if he could have another chance

95

To teach him how to build a load of hay—'

'I know, that's Silas' one accomplishment.
He bundles every forkful in its place,
And tags and numbers it for future reference,   90
So he can find and easily dislodge it
In the unloading. Silas does that well.
He takes it out in bunches like big birds' nests.
You never see him standing on the hay
He's trying to lift, straining to lift himself.'   95

'He thinks if he could teach him that, he'd be
Some good perhaps to someone in the world.
He hates to see a boy the fool of books.
Poor Silas, so concerned for other folk,
And nothing to look backward to with pride,   100
And nothing to look forward to with hope,
So now and never any different.'

Part of a moon was falling down the west,
Dragging the whole sky with it to the hills.
Its light poured softly in her lap. She saw it   105
And spread her apron to it. She put out her hand
Among the harp-like morning-glory strings,
Taut with the dew from garden bed to eaves,
As if she played unheard some tenderness
That wrought on him beside her in the night.   110
'Warren,' she said, 'he has come home to die:
You needn't be afraid he'll leave you this time.'

'Home,' he mocked gently.

                              'Yes, what else but home?
It all depends on what you mean by home.
Of course he's nothing to us, any more   115
Than was the hound that came a stranger to us
Out of the woods, worn out upon the trail.'

'Home is the place where, when you have to go
    there,
They have to take you in.'

                              'I should have called it
Something you somehow haven't to deserve.'   120

Warren leaned out and took a step or two,
Picked up a little stick, and brought it back
And broke it in his hand and tossed it by.
'Silas has better claim on us you think
Than on his brother? Thirteen little miles   125
As the road winds would bring him to his door.
Silas has walked that far no doubt today.
Why didn't he go there? His brother's rich,
A somebody—director in the bank.'

'He never told us that.'

                              'We know it though.'   130

'I think his brother ought to help, of course.
I'll see to that if there is need. He ought of right
To take him in, and might be willing to—
He may be better than appearances.
But have some pity on Silas. Do you think   135
If he had any pride in claiming kin
Or anything he looked for from his brother,
He'd keep so still about him all this time?'

'I wonder what's between them.'

                              'I can tell you.
Silas is what he is—we wouldn't mind him—   140
But just the kind that kinsfolk can't abide.
He never did a thing so very bad.
He don't know why he isn't quite as good
As anybody. Worthless though he is,

He won't be made ashamed to please his brother.' ¹⁴⁵

'*I* can't think Si ever hurt anyone.'

'No, but he hurt my heart the way he lay
And rolled his old head on that sharp-edged
    chairback.
He wouldn't let me put him on the lounge.
You must go in and see what you can do.   150
I made the bed up for him there tonight.
You'll be surprised at him—how much he's broken.
His working days are done; I'm sure of it.'

'I'd not be in a hurry to say that.'

'I haven't been. Go, look, see for yourself.   155
But, Warren, please remember how it is:
He's come to help you ditch the meadow.
He has a plan. You mustn't laugh at him.
He may not speak of it, and then he may.
I'll sit and see if that small sailing cloud   160
Will hit or miss the moon.'

                        It hit the moon.
Then there were three there, making a dim row,
The moon, the little silver cloud, and she.

Warren returned—too soon, it seemed to her,
Slipped to her side, caught up her hand and
    waited.   165

'Warren?' she questioned.

                        'Dead,' was all he answered.

This long dramatic dialogue gives Frost an opportunity to explore the theme of work in even greater depth, relating it to the basic questions of a man's integrity and self-respect, his place in the world, and his claims on his fellow-men. The title gives us a clue to the poem's urgency: at the point of death, a man's entire life is being summed up and weighed. Silas may seem a very humble example for Frost to choose, but in him we can look at human existence stripped bare of all but the essentials. The movement of the poem is relaxed and conversational, yet each detail opens up a new perspective on the problems Frost is concerned with.

How much does a man have to "deserve" or "earn" in life? This is the question that divides Mary and Warren from the beginning. Mary argues with compassion that simply because Silas is a human being, and because they have sheltered him for many winters in the past, they have a moral obligation to provide him with a "home." To Mary, this is "something you somehow haven't to deserve" (line 120). Even though she knows Silas can no longer work, she does not call his bluff when he talks of the improvements he will make on the farm; she understands his reluctance to ask for charity. Considering Frost's characterization of Mary as a whole, why do you think he makes such a point of relating her to the moon (lines 103–106, 160–163)?

Warren takes a more hard-headed, common-sense position. At the beginning of the poem, he sees Silas only as a "hired man," and as such he is nearly worthless—weak, undependable, ready to be lured away during the haying season by some neighbor who offers pocket money. Can you trace the stages of Warren's movement towards a gentler, more understanding mood? Notice in particular the lines in which Warren describes Silas' one outstanding accomplishment: he can stack a hay wagon superbly (lines 88–95). It is the kind of job well done that wins Warren's (and Frost's) wholehearted respect.

And this, we discover, is the accomplishment that stands out in Silas' jumbled mind, as well. It might seem a small thing for a man to stake his whole identity on, but then, building forkful by forkful a well-formed load of hay is not so different from building word by word a well-formed poem. It is the fundamental act of giving form, which, for Frost, represented "a momentary stay against the confusion of the world."

Building a hay load is the skill the hired man most wanted to pass on to the college student Harold Wilson:

'He thinks if he could teach him that, he'd be
Some good perhaps to someone in the world.' (96–97)

Why do you think Silas' summer-long argument with Harold Wilson so obsesses him now, four years later? What was the boy's attitude towards his own kind of work—studying? Do you think he and Silas had anything in common?

We never see Silas directly in the poem, but it reveals a good deal about his own motives and estimate of himself. Why, for instance, doesn't he go to his brother's house for help? Do you think he would prefer to judge himself from Mary's or Warren's point of view? Is it significant that it is Warren, rather than Mary, who finds him and reports his death?

Men Work Together

Self-help. Helping each other. The issue is drawn between them. *Nearly all my poetry has something to do
with that.*[67]

The next two poems should be read together, in light
of this statement made by Frost in 1957. The poems do
not divide simply on each side of the issue. "The Tuft
of Flowers" describes a lone individual, yet he is working with someone; while "Mending Wall" describes
two people working together, yet in many ways alone.
Both poems can be read as political tracts, social analyses, or a poet's views on the way men relate to each
other and to their work.

There has been a pattern in this book so far: the
response to malicious nature is courage. Courage shows
itself through enduring, and the job of work gives
meaning to endurance. Now, we must consider how the
work is to be done: do we work together—or alone?

THE TUFT OF FLOWERS

I went to turn the grass once after one
Who mowed it in the dew before the sun.

The dew was gone that made his blade so keen
Before I came to view the leveled scene.

I looked for him behind an isle of trees;   5
I listened for his whetstone on the breeze.

But he had gone his way, the grass all mown,
And I must be, as he had been,—alone,

'As all must be,' I said within my heart,
'Whether they work together or apart.'   10

But as I said it, swift there passed me by
On noiseless wing a bewildered butterfly,

Seeking with memories grown dim o'er night
Some resting flower of yesterday's delight.

And once I marked his flight go round and round,   15
As where some flower lay withering on the
    ground.

And then he flew as far as eye could see,
And then on tremulous wing came back to me.

I thought of questions that have no reply,
And would have turned to toss the grass to dry;   20

But he turned first, and led my eye to look
At a tall tuft of flowers beside a brook,

A leaping tongue of bloom the scythe had spared
Beside a reedy brook the scythe had bared.

The mower in the dew had loved them thus,   25
By leaving them to flourish, not for us,

Nor yet to draw one thought of ours to him,
But from sheer morning gladness at the brim.

The butterfly and I had lit upon,
Nevertheless, a message from the dawn,　　　30

That made me hear the wakening birds around,
And hear his long scythe whispering to the
　ground,

And feel a spirit kindred to my own;
So that henceforth I worked no more alone;

But glad with him, I worked as with his aid,　　35
And weary, sought at noon with him the shade;

And dreaming, as it were, held brotherly speech
With one whose thought I had not hoped to
　reach.

'Men work together,' I told him from the heart,
'Whether they work together or apart.'　　40

The disappointed butterfly, searching for flowers in the
mown field, finally discovers a tuft of flowers still standing. Why were these flowers spared, and why does this
discovery change the speaker's mind about the essential
loneliness of all men (lines 7–10)? In what sense are there
two men working together in the field?

Considering all of Frost's poetry that you have read
and thought about, do you think that the speaker is stat-
ing a fact in the last stanza, or is it only a hope he cher-
ishes?

MENDING WALL

Something there is that doesn't love a wall,
That sends the frozen-ground-swell under it,
And spills the upper boulders in the sun;
And makes gaps even two can pass abreast.
The work of hunters is another thing: 5
I have come after them and made repair
Where they have left not one stone on a stone,
But they would have the rabbit out of hiding,
To please the yelping dogs. The gaps I mean,
No one has seen them made or heard them made,   10
But at spring mending-time we find them there.
I let my neighbor know beyond the hill;
And on a day we meet to walk the line
And set the wall between us once again.
We keep the wall between us as we go.   15
To each the boulders that have fallen to each.
And some are loaves and some so nearly balls
We have to use a spell to make them balance:
'Stay where you are until our backs are turned!'
We wear our fingers rough with handling them.   20
Oh, just another kind of outdoor game,
One on a side. It comes to little more:
There where it is we do not need the wall:
He is all pine and I am apple orchard.
My apple trees will never get across   25
And eat the cones under his pines, I tell him.
He only says, 'Good fences make good
    neighbors.'
Spring is the mischief in me, and I wonder
If I could put a notion in his head:
'*Why* do they make good neighbors? Isn't it   30
Where there are cows? But here there are no
    cows.

Before I built a wall I'd ask to know
What I was walling in or walling out,
And to whom I was like to give offense.
Something there is that doesn't love a wall,   35
That wants it down.' I could say 'Elves' to him,
But it's not elves exactly, and I'd rather
He said it for himself. I see him there
Bringing a stone grasped firmly by the top
In each hand, like an old-stone savage armed.   40
He moves in darkness as it seems to me,
Not of woods only and the shade of trees.
He will not go behind his father's saying,
And he likes having thought of it so well
He says again, 'Good fences make good
    neighbors.'   45

Much of the public knows Frost by the phrase "Good fences make good neighbors." But the speaker in "Mending Wall" is saying just the opposite: that there is some mysterious force at work to break down barriers between human beings. "Elves," he calls it, in contrast to the matter-of-fact damage done by hunters (lines 5–11). But this is only a hint of what each person must discover for himself—companionship, respect, love, or the mystical togetherness of men who work.

The speaker's description of his neighbor makes the point even clearer (lines 38–42). The man and his ideas still belong to stone-age savagery. The darkness which surrounds him is not simply the natural darkness of the woods, but the primordial destructiveness in the heart of man. There is darkness also in the conventional mentality that makes a man repeat "Good fences make good neighbors" simply because his father said it (lines 43–44), when it does not fit the new situation at all (lines 30–31).

The poem, however, illustrates the difficulty of making a definite statement about any of Frost's ideas. The speaker does not agree with his neighbor in theory (lines 23–36); but, in the fact of his labor, he is doing the same thing his neighbor is doing. Can you reconcile the speaker's thoughts with his actions? Are the questions raised by "Mending Wall" and by "The Tuft of Flowers" still relevant in today's global society? Can you apply them to some contemporary issue?

4 Making a Poem

The Speaking Voice

Any psychiatrist will tell you that making a basket, or making a horseshoe, or giving anything form gives you a confidence in the universe . . . that it has form, see. When you talk about your troubles and go to somebody about them, you're just a fool. The best way to settle them is to make something that has form, because all you want to do is get a sense of form.[68]

For Frost it was poetry that gave the necessary "sense of form." Since it was form that interested him, and not simply the expression of his feelings about the world, it's not surprising that Frost should have very definite ideas about the techniques of poetry. Frost had a great deal to say on this subject, but his main principles can be summed up in this way:

1. Poetry is a pattern of sound.
2. A poem is a dramatic event.
3. "Poetry is the art of saying one thing and meaning one thing more—at least one."

This section will show how Frost uses these three principles as his tools for making a poem.

Poetry: a pattern of sound

It would seem absurd to say it (and you mustn't quote me as saying it), but I suppose the fact is that my conscious interest in people was at first no more than an almost technical interest *in their speech—in what I used to call their sentence sounds—the sound of sense* [italics added]. Whatever these sounds are or aren't (they are certainly not of the vowels and consonants of words nor even of the words themselves, but something the words are—chiefly a kind of notation for indicating and fastening to the printed page), whatever they are, I say, I began to hang on them very young. I was under twenty when I deliberately put it to myself, one night after good conversation, that there are moments when we actually touch in talk what the best writing can only come near. The curse of our book language is not so much that it keeps forever to the same set phrases (though Heaven knows those are bad enough), but that it sounds forever with the same reading tones. We must go back into the vernacular for tones that haven't been brought to book. We must write with the ear on the speaking voice. We must imagine the speaking voice.[69]

. . . I alone of English writers have consciously set myself to make music out of what I may call the sound of sense. Now it is possible to have sense without the sound of sense (as in much prose that is supposed to pass muster but makes very dull reading) and the sound of sense without sense (as in *Alice in Wonderland*, which makes anything but dull reading). The best place to get the abstract sound of sense is from voices behind a door that cuts off the words. Ask yourself how these sentences would sound without the words in which they are embodied:

> You mean to tell me you can't read?
> I said no such thing.
> Well, read then.
> You're not my teacher.[70]

With Frost's idea in mind, read the following two stanzas from William McGonagall's "An Autumn Reverie." Then reread Frost's "Reluctance" (p. 66), and compare stanzas 2 and 3 with McGonagall's poem. Notice particularly how Frost combines the poetic rhythms with normal speech patterns, while McGonagall sticks doggedly to the rhythm furnished by the words themselves.

> Alas! beautiful Summer now hath fled,
> And the face of Nature doth seem dead,
> And the leaves are withered, and falling off the
>   trees,
> By the nipping and chilling autumnal breeze.

> The pleasures of the little birds are all fled,
> And with the cold many of them will be found dead,
> Because the leaves of the trees are scattered in the
>   blast,
> And makes the feathered creatures feel downcast.

Here is Frost's own explanation of the difference between two poems such as these:

> If one is to be a poet he must learn to get cadences by skillfully breaking the sounds of sense with all their irregularity of accent across the regular beat of the meter. Verse in which there is nothing but the beat of the meter furnished by the accents of the polysyllabic words we call doggerel. Verse is not that. Neither is it the sound of sense alone. It is a resultant from those two.[71]

Below are two sets of passages. In each set, label each passage as doggerel, sound of sense, or the perfect combination—Frost's poetry.

a) Everyone has heard this bird sing in mid-summer.
   He is loud and makes the wood ring, by knocking
   Against the solid tree trunks.

   There is a singer everyone has heard,
   Loud, a mid-summer and mid-wood bird,
   Who makes the solid-tree trunks sound again.

   In summer all have heard the sing
   Of mid-wood birds that make woods ring.
   The branches of the trees will sway
   As mid-wood birds make noise all day.

b) Snow falling and night falling fast, oh, fast
   In a field I looked into going past,
   And the ground almost covered smooth in snow,
   But a few weeds and stubble showing last.

   The snow and night were coming fast
   In fields I saw while going past.
   The ground was almost covered now.
   Except for weeds that I saw last.

   The snow was falling pretty fast
   As I drove home going past
   That field; and the ground was almost covered
   Except for a few weeds. I saw those last.

Try rewriting a passage from a Frost poem as either pure prose or pure metrical verse. Or, if you feel inspired, take the following prose passage from one of Frost's letters, and see if you can form it into poetry without getting doggerel.

There's a vigorous devil in me that raises me above or drops me below the level of pity. Nevertheless, I sometimes weep internally with sorrow (but not as often as externally at the eyes with cold weather).[72]

Poetry: the dramatic necessity

Frost's second principle is that:

A dramatic necessity goes deep into the nature of the sentence. Sentences are not different enough to hold the attention unless they are dramatic. No ingenuity of varying structure will do. All that can save them is the speaking tone of voice somehow entangled in the words and fastened to the page for the ear of the imagination. That is all that can save poetry from singsong, all that can save prose from itself.[73]

PROVIDE, PROVIDE

The witch that came (the withered hag)
To wash the steps with pail and rag,
Was once the beauty Abishag,

The picture pride of Hollywood.
Too many fall from great and good   5
For you to doubt the likelihood.

Die early and avoid the fate.
Or if predestined to die late,
Make up your mind to die in state.

Make the whole stock exchange your own!   10
If need be occupy a throne,
Where nobody can call *you* crone.

Some have relied on what they knew;
Others on being simply true.
What worked for them might work for you.   15

No memory of having starred
Atones for later disregard,
Or keeps the end from being hard.

Better to go down dignified
With boughten friendship at your side   20
Than none at all. Provide, provide!

Frost suggests several different ways to provide for old age: you can amass money ("the whole stock exchange") or power ("a throne") or knowledge—or you can simply be "true" (presumably to others and to yourself). Which methods are most often chosen in our society? On which would you place your reliance? How important is it to "go down dignified"?

The "sound of sense"—the dramatic tone of voice—may help you decide how Frost wanted you to take this poem. Read the poem aloud. Notice the hard rhyme, the exaggerated meter, and the blunt title. What do they all mean? The poem sounds cynical and hypocritical—certainly not like the Frost most readers know. Perhaps there was a twinkle in his eye as he wondered if people would fall for such a mercenary philosophy. What do you think?

Frost's third principle is that poetry begins and ends in metaphor in an attempt to say one thing in terms of something else, that is, to represent abstract ideas by concrete images. One must remember, though, that words themselves are but metaphors for things. We can think of them as simply the symbols which we have agreed upon in order to communicate with each other.

> Poetry provides the one permissible way of saying one thing and meaning another. People say, "Why don't you say what you mean?" We never do that, do we, being all of us too much poets. We like to talk in parables and in hints and in indirections—whether from diffidence or some other instinct.
>
> I have wanted in late years to go further and further in making metaphor the whole of thinking. I find someone now and then to agree with me that all thinking, except mathematical thinking, is metaphorical, or all thinking except scientific thinking.[74]

Now that you are aware of Frost's dependence on metaphor, look at the early version of "Nothing Gold Can Stay" which follows. Below it is the final version which he published.

Nature's first green is gold,
Her hardest hue to hold.
Her early leaves are flowers;
But only so for hours.
Then leaves subside to leaves.   5
In autumn she achieves
A still more golden blaze.
But nothing golden stays.

NOTHING GOLD CAN STAY

Nature's first green is gold,
Her hardest hue to hold.
Her early leaf's a flower;
But only so an hour.
Then leaf subsides to leaf.   5
So Eden sank to grief,
So dawn goes down to day.
Nothing gold can stay.

This is a good example of how a poet works to clarify and strengthen the central idea of his poem through metaphor. If Frost was trying to express his feeling of "diminished things," why do you think he discarded lines 6–7 of the original? How do the two added metaphors in the final version reinforce his theme?

In addition to expressing an idea concretely and vividly, metaphors can expand the significance of a poem by bringing in different areas of reality. Which of Frost's metaphors here extends the meaning of the poem beyond the seasonal cycle into the realm of man and God?

By the time the last line is reached, the word "gold" itself has become a metaphor for countless moments and feelings. What might some of them be?

Working From an Original Manuscript

Anyone who has investigated what a poem says and the form it takes to say it has wondered just how hard it was for the poet to write it exactly in that way. Did he struggle to get every word just right or was it created nearly perfect from inspiration?

Here is one of Frost's most famous poems. After reading it and answering the questions for further understanding, turn to the photograph of his manuscript on p. 123, and see if you can determine some of the steps Frost used in turning an experience or an idea into the form of poetry.

STOPPING BY WOODS
ON A SNOWY EVENING

Whose woods these are I think I know.
His house is in the village though;
He will not see me stopping here
To watch his woods fill up with snow.

My little horse must think it queer   5
To stop without a farmhouse near
Between the woods and frozen lake
The darkest evening of the year.

He gives his harness bells a shake
To ask if there is some mistake.   10
The only other sound's the sweep
Of easy wind and downy flake.

The woods are lovely, dark and deep,
But I have promises to keep,
And miles to go before I sleep,   15
And miles to go before I sleep.

1 What vowel sound is stressed through repetition in the first stanza? Say this sound aloud several times. What feelings does it suggest?

2 What is the poem's rhyme scheme?

3 There is, perhaps, a very subtle suggestion in the first stanza that ownership of the woods exists on more than one level. Who owns these woods: the speaker who is getting such intense feelings from watching them or the man who lives in town?

4 Frost has endured much ribbing for having "little horses who think" in his poems. One realizes, however, that the speaker is whimsically giving through the horse the ideas that might be expressed by townsmen if they were present. What would the owner of the woods probably say? Could the owner, then, represent horse sense?

5 To make stopping more irrational and lacking in good sense (in contrast to hurrying on home in such bleak, stormy weather), what details emphasize how bad the time and place are for stopping? Find at least four.

6 What two sounds are mentioned in the poem? Which one is more imagined than actual—as if half-dreamed while falling asleep?

7 Frost has said that a poem is a way of saying one thing while meaning something else. If this poem is about something more than a scenic stop of a tired man, what could the woods represent?

8 Which of the following best describes the repetition of the last line?
   a) It is simply a tired man repeating himself.
   b) A decision is being made in one line and regret for a course not taken is being expressed in the other. (If this is so, which line is decision and which is regret?)
   c) One line emphasizes the word "miles" and the other emphasizes "sleep."
   Or is there a fourth alternative?

[Please note that the manuscript contains only the last three stanzas. The first stanza was identical in manuscript and final version.]

1 Frost has said that the first stanza of the finished poem came quickly and easily to him. But what evidence is there in his attempts to begin the second stanza that the actual incident was not as clear in his mind?

2 What is gained by having "my little horse" be the speaker's only company in the storm instead of "steaming horses"?

3 In "Nothing Gold Can Stay" (p. 116), Frost revised usually from the abstract to the more concrete and from literal detail to metaphor. (Are these generally good rules in revising creative writing?) Where in the three stanzas has he done these two things?

4 Why did Frost change the sex of the horse from male to female in the manuscript and then back again for the final printing? We may never agree on the answer, but it is an interesting insight into an artist's roads not taken when writing.

5 There has been a great deal written about Frost's genius in ending with repeating lines, but Frost himself seemed to feel it was simply a good poetic trick:

> Then for a small chaser of the lowdown, under the head perhaps of curiosa, I might confess the trade secret that I wrote the third line of the last stanza of "Stopping by Woods" in such a way as to call for another stanza when I didn't want another stanza and didn't have another stanza in me, but with great presence of mind and a sense of what a good boy I was I instantly struck the line out and made my exit with a repeat end.[76]

This letter introduces one of the most argued concepts of creativity. Someone has said that genius is ten percent inspiration and ninety percent perspiration. Can you tell by the above letter and by your knowledge of how Frost wrote his poems if this statement would apply to him? What do you think constitutes creative genius?

The ~~steaming~~ ~~horses think it queer~~

To ~~will~~ have must

The ~~horse~~ ~~begins~~ to think it queer

To
We stop without a farm house near

                    the woods in a frozen
Between a ~~forest~~ ~~and a~~ lake

The darkest evening of the year

      She   her
~~He~~ gives harness bells a shake

To ask if there is some mistake

                            the
The only other sounds the ~~swish~~

                          downy
Of easy wind and ~~fall of~~ flake.

The woods are lovely dark and deep

But I have promises to keep

~~That bid me ~~in my~~ ~~and there are miles,~~~~ ~~give ~~the ~~miles a ~~sleeting~~~~

And miles to go before I sleep

And miles to go before I sleep[74]

And were an epitaph to be my story
I'd have a short one ready for my own.
I would have written of me on my stone:
I had a lover's quarrel with the world.[77]

NOTES

1 Robert Frost, from a taped speech given at The Choate School, Wallingford, Conn., for the dedication of the school's Andrew Mellon Library, May 5, 1962.

2 John Sherrill, "An Interview with Robert Frost," *Guideposts*, August, 1955, p. 5.

3 John Ciardi, "Robert Frost: To Earthward," *Saturday Review*, February 23, 1963, p. 24.

4 WGBH Educational Foundation and Holt, Rinehart and Winston, Inc., *A Lover's Quarrel with the World* (film), New York: Holt, Rinehart and Winston, Inc., 1963.

5 *The Letters of Robert Frost to Louis Untermeyer*, New York: Holt, Rinehart and Winston, Inc., 1963, p. 376.

6 Margaret Bartlett Anderson, *Robert Frost and John Bartlett: The Record of a Friendship*, New York: Holt, Rinehart and Winston, Inc., 1963, p. 153.

7 Edward Connery Lathem, ed., *Interviews with Robert Frost*, New York: Holt, Rinehart and Winston, Inc., 1966, p. 90.

8 Lawrance Thompson, *Robert Frost: The Early Years 1874-1915*, New York: Holt, Rinehart and Winston, Inc., 1966, pp. 39-40.

9 WGBH, *op. cit.*

10 Elizabeth Shepley Sergeant, *Robert Frost: The Trial by Existence*, New York: Holt, Rinehart and Winston, Inc., 1960, p. 22.

11 *Ibid.*, p. 23.

12 Lathem, *op. cit.*, p. 36.

13 Sergeant, *op. cit.*, pp. 26-27.

14 *Ibid.*, p. 14.

15 *Ibid.*, pp. 29-30.

16 Lawrance Thompson, ed., *Selected Letters of Robert Frost*, New York: Holt, Rinehart and Winston, Inc., 1964, p. 16.

17 Sergeant, *op. cit.*, p. 35.

18 *Ibid.*, p. 48.

19 *Ibid.*, p. 54.

20 *Letters to Louis Untermeyer*, *op. cit.*, p. 353.

21 Sergeant, *op. cit.*, p. 55.

22 Thompson, *The Early Years*, *op. cit.*, pp. 265-266.

23 WGBH, *op. cit.*

24 Thompson, *The Early Years*, *op. cit.*, p. 267.

25 *Ibid.*, p. 274.

26 Thompson, *Selected Letters*, *op. cit.*, "Letter to Robert Chase, March 4, 1952," p. 552.

27 Anderson, *op. cit.*, pp. 4-5.

28 *Ibid.*, p. 6.

29 *Ibid.*, p. 7.

30 Thompson, *Selected Letters, op. cit.*, "Letter to Robert Chase, March 4, 1952," pp. 551–552.

31 Anderson, *op. cit.*, pp. 8–9.

32 *Ibid.*, p. 10.

33 *Ibid.*, pp. 11–12.

34 Sergeant, *op. cit.*, pp. 88–89.

35 Thompson, *Selected Letters, op. cit.*, pp. 53–54.

36 Sergeant, *op. cit.*, p. 97.

37 Lathem, *op. cit.*, pp. 37–38.

38 *Ibid.*, p. 22.

39 Anderson, *op. cit.*, pp. 51–52.

40 Thompson, *Selected Letters, op. cit.*, pp. 50–51.

41 WGBH, *op. cit.*

42 Thompson, *Selected Letters, op. cit.*, p. 51.

43 *Ibid.*, p. 126.

44 Sergeant, *op. cit.*, "Letter to Sidney Cox, August 20, 1914," pp. 139–140.

45 Alfred Harcourt, *Some Experiences*, privately printed by Alfred and Ellen Harcourt, Riverside, Conn., 1951, pp. 21–22.

46 Thompson, *Selected Letters, op. cit.*, pp. 158–160.

47 Sergeant, *op. cit.*, p. 185.

48 *Letters to Louis Untermeyer, op. cit.*, p. 307.

49 *Ibid.*, pp. 295–296.

50 Thompson, *Selected Letters, op. cit.*, pp. 470–471.

51 *Letters to Louis Untermeyer, op. cit.*, pp. 378–379.

52 Thompson, *Selected Letters, op. cit.*, p. 596.

53 Ciardi, *op. cit.*, p. 24.

54 Thompson, *Selected Letters, op. cit.*, "Letter to Leonidas W. Payne, Jr., November 1, 1927," p. 344.

55 Robert Frost, "From Iron," *In the Clearing*, New York: Holt, Rinehart and Winston, Inc., 1962, p. 95.

56 Sergeant, *op. cit.*, p. 304.

57 Thompson, *Selected Letters, op. cit.*, "Letter to Lincoln MacVeagh, November 19, 1923," p. 296.

58 WGBH, *op. cit.*

59 Dylan Thomas, "Do Not Go Gentle into That Good Night," *Collected Poems*, New York: New Directions Publishing Corporation, 1957.

60 Marion Montgomery, "Robert Frost and His Use of Barriers: Man vs. Nature Toward God," *South Atlantic Quarterly*, 1958.

61 Cleanth Brooks and Robert Penn Warren, "Letter from Robert Frost," as quoted in *Understanding Poetry*, 3rd ed., New York: Holt, Rinehart and Winston, Inc., 1960, p. 524.

62 WGBH, *op. cit.*

63 *Ibid.*

64 *Ibid.*

65 Thompson, *Selected Letters, op. cit.*, "Letter to Thomas Mosher, July 17, 1913," p. 83.

66 WGBH, *op. cit.*

67 Sergeant, *op. cit.*, p. 406.

68 WGBH, *op. cit.*

69 Thompson, *Selected Letters, op. cit.*, "Letter to William Stanley Braithwaite, March 22, 1915," pp. 158–159.

70 *Ibid.*, "Letter to John T. Bartlett, July 4, 1913," pp. 79–81.

71 *Ibid.*, pp. 80–81.

72 *Ibid.*, "Letter to Louis Untermeyer, November 28, 1938," p. 483.

73 Sergeant, *op. cit.*, p. 222.

74 Hyde Cox and Edward Connery Lathem, eds., "Education by Poetry," *Selected Prose of Robert Frost*, New York: Holt, Rinehart and Winston, Inc., 1966, pp. 36–37.

75 Robert Frost, facsimile of the last three stanzas of "Stopping by Woods on a Snowy Evening," New York: Holt, Rinehart and Winston, Inc.

76 Brooks and Warren, *op. cit.*, "Letter to Charles Madison, February 26, 1950," p. 524.

77 Robert Frost, "The Lesson for Today," *Complete Poems of Robert Frost*, New York: Holt, Rinehart and Winston, Inc., 1949, p. 471.

Annotated Bibliography

POETRY:

FROST, ROBERT. *Complete Poems of Robert Frost.* New York: Holt, Rinehart and Winston, Inc., 1949.

FROST, ROBERT. *In the Clearing.* New York: Holt, Rinehart and Winston, Inc., 1962.

FOR FURTHER READING:

ANDERSON, MARGARET BARTLETT, *Robert Frost and John Bartlett: The Record of a Friendship.* New York: Holt, Rinehart and Winston, Inc., 1963.

An account of a lifelong friendship between Frost and a former student, based on letters, notes, and personal experiences of the author with Frost.

COX, HYDE, and EDWARD CONNERY LATHEM, eds.

Selected Prose of Robert Frost. New York: Holt, Rinehart and Winston, Inc., 1966.

A collection of Frost's most significant prose pieces, interesting because he rarely wrote prose articles.

COX, JAMES M., ed. *Robert Frost: A Collection of Critical Essays* (Twentieth Century Views). Englewood Cliffs: Prentice-Hall, Inc., 1962.

The most complete collection of critical articles on Frost and his thoughts with a few articles on specific poems.

FROST, ROBERT. *The Letters of Robert Frost to Louis Untermeyer*. New York: Holt, Rinehart and Winston, Inc., 1963.

A record of a friendship and a portrait of Frost and his thinking. It covers the period from 1915 to 1961, with Untermeyer's commentary.

GREENBERG, ROBERT A., and JAMES G. HEPBURN, eds. *Robert Frost: An Introduction*. New York: Holt, Rinehart and Winston, Inc., 1961.

A short paperback containing an anthology of Frost's poems, short selections from many authors analyzing selected poems, and a useful collection of critical articles.

LATHEM, EDWARD CONNERY, ed. *Interviews with Robert Frost*. New York: Holt, Rinehart and Winston, Inc., 1966.

An excellent collection of interviews covering the period from 1915 to 1962.

SERGEANT, ELIZABETH SHEPLEY. *Robert Frost: The Trial by Existence*. New York: Holt, Rinehart and Winston, Inc., 1960.

A biography containing many revealing statements by the poet to the author.

THOMPSON, LAWRANCE. *Fire and Ice: The Art and Thought of Robert Frost*. New York: Russell & Russell Publishers, 1961.

This rates among the best poem-by-poem analyses of Frost's work for the beginning student, but it does not include the last period of Frost's writing life.

THOMPSON, LAWRANCE. *Robert Frost: The Early Years, 1874–1915*. New York: Holt, Rinehart and Winston, Inc., 1966.

The official biography, covering the period from Frost's boyhood in California to his return from England. A second volume is in preparation.

THOMPSON, LAWRANCE, ed. *Selected Letters of Robert Frost*. New York: Holt, Rinehart and Winston, Inc., 1964.

An extensive collection of Frost's letters, containing a chronology and genealogy and an excellent introduction by Thompson.

FOR LISTENING:

BROOKS, CLEANTH, and ROBERT PENN WARREN. *Conversations on the Craft of Poetry*. New York: Holt, Rinehart and Winston, Inc., 1961.

A tape recording and accompanying transcript in which Frost and three other poets talk informally about metrical and rhythmical problems in writing poetry.

FROST, LESLEY. *Derry Down Derry*. New York: Folkways Record & Service Corp., FL9733, 1961.

A recording of Frost's daughter reading some of his poetry, with commentary about life on the farm at Derry, N.H.

FROST, ROBERT. *Robert Frost Reads from His Own Works: Yale Series of Recorded Poets*. New York: Decca Records, a division of MCA Inc., DL9127, 1966.

Especially interesting because of comments by Frost as he introduces and reads his poems.

FROST, ROBERT. *Robert Frost Reads His Poetry*. New York: Caedmon Records, Inc., TC1060, 1957.

A varied collection of his works, including a brilliant reading of "The Witch of Coos."

NOTE

A somewhat different version of this book is available from Holt, Rinehart and Winston, Inc., 383 Madison Avenue, New York, N.Y. 10017. It contains two previously uncollected poems and one previously unpublished poem, "One Favored Acorn" (not included in this edition), and a seven-inch, 33⅓ record of Frost reading eight of his poems inserted in the back cover. Seven of the poems on the record are readings that have not been recorded elsewhere.

A FILM ABOUT ROBERT FROST

Also available for classroom use is the Academy Award-winning documentary film *Robert Frost: A Lover's Quarrel with the World*, by Robert Hughes and Charlotte Zwerin (black and white, 39 minutes). Made shortly before Frost's death, it shows him going about ordinary tasks at his cabin near Ripton, Vermont, giving a poetry reading at Sarah Lawrence College, talking with a group of students at Amherst, and in Washington receiving a medal from President Kennedy. Frost tells the story of his early years in his own words, voices some of his trenchant opinions about poetry, education, and life in general, and reads several of his poems, including "Away," "In Winter in the Woods Alone," "The Objection to Being Stepped On," "Provide, Provide," and "Dust of Snow." Many of the themes emphasized in this book are threaded throughout the film.

Reviewing the film in *Media and Methods*, Kirby Judd wrote:

> Through the film runs humor: people laugh and smile with him, or he laughs at himself. Yet, behind the smile there is seriousness—the feeling that he is alone even among the attentive students. As he speaks and pauses, his mind seems to be playing with other ideas that he is not telling us about. The complexity of his personality is evident.

A Lover's Quarrel with the World can be rented from several audio-visual libraries, and it can be previewed and purchased from Holt, Rinehart and Winston, Inc.

Acknowledgments

The authors and editors wish to thank the following authors, publishers, libraries, and artists for use of copyrighted or privately owned material.

THE AMHERST GRADUATES' QUARTERLY, Amherst College, for excerpt from "Education by Poetry," a talk delivered by Robert Frost at Amherst College and subsequently revised for publication in *The Amherst Graduates' Quarterly* of February, 1931.

THE BOSTON TRAVELER for excerpt from an interview article by Paul Waitt, which appeared in the *Traveler* on April 11, 1921.

THE BURLINGTON FREE PRESS for excerpt from an interview article, which appeared in the *Free Press and Times* on August 19, 1936.

THE CHOATE SCHOOL for excerpt from a taped speech given at

133

NEW DIRECTIONS PUBLISHING CORPORATION for two lines from "Do Not Go Gentle into That Good Night" by Dylan Thomas from *The Collected Poems of Dylan Thomas*, copyright 1953 by Dylan Thomas, copyright © 1957 by New Directions; J. M. Dent & Sons, Ltd., from *The Collected Poems of Dylan Thomas*, copyright 1953 by Dylan Thomas, copyright © 1957 by J. M. Dent & Sons, Ltd. and the Literary Executors of The Dylan Thomas Estate.

SATURDAY REVIEW for excerpts from John Ciardi's editorial "Robert Frost: To Earthward," in *Saturday Review*, February 23, 1963.

SOUTH ATLANTIC QUARTERLY for excerpts from "Robert Frost and His Use of Barriers: Man vs. Nature Toward God," by Marion Montgomery in *South Atlantic Quarterly*, 1958.

UNIVERSITY OF MICHIGAN for excerpt from "Notes from Conversations with Robert Frost," by M. P. Tilly, which appeared in *The Inlander* for February, 1918.

WGBH EDUCATIONAL FOUNDATION and HOLT, RINEHART AND WINSTON, INC. for *A Lover's Quarrel with the World* (film) 1963, produced by WGBH Educational Foundation, Boston, Mass. and Holt, Rinehart and Winston, Inc., New York. Copyright © 1963 by Holt, Rinehart and Winston, Inc.

WIDE WORLD PHOTOS for photograph on page 30.

Lastly, we would like to personally thank MR. NEWTON MC-KEON of the Robert Frost Library at Amherst College, MR. CHARLES GREEN and MR. WILLIAM MERRILL of The Jones Library in Amherst, and MR. EDWARD CONNERY LATHEM and MR. KENNETH CRAMER of the Baker Library at Dartmouth College for their patience and kind assistance in locating photographic and other materials that appear in this book.